THE PARLOUR CAFÉ COOKBOOK

by Gillian Veal

First published in Scotland in 2011 by Kitchen Press
1 Windsor Place, Dundee, DD2 1BG
Reprinted 2011, 2012, 2014

Designed & typeset by Anti Limited

www.hellojenuine.com

www.anti-limited.com

A CIP catalogue record for this book is available from the British Library.

ISBN 978-0-9570373-0-4

Printed and bound in the UK by Martins the Printers Ltd.

I would like to dedicate this book to my late father, Francis Agley, who loved his food.

Acknowledgements

Thanks to my family, especially my mum and Tam Maxfield, for all their support; to the whole team at The Parlour, past and present; to my business partner Lesley Tierney; and to all our customers, as without them there would be no business.

Thanks also to the following people, who have all made valuable contributions to this book one way or the other: Joby Catto, Jen Collins, James Drury, Peter Mansfield, Emanuele Castaldo, Alison Keeble from the Yellow Door Bakery, Scot Herbs, Anna Day, Zoe Venditozzi, Hilary Scott Buchanan, Ellie Johnson and Maxine Clark.

Also a special thanks to Emily Dewhurst, my publisher, for giving me the opportunity, the confidence and the gentle nudging to write and finish the book.

Contents

BURSTING WITH PARLOUR FLAVOUR

Introduction

I started The Parlour Café in December 2005, fresh back from London and in need of a job. The Parlour was just a combination of everything I'd done to that point, all the odd jobs, all the little bars I'd worked in, the random restaurants and the chefs I learned from, the places I'd eaten and the markets I'd walked through. There was a huge gap in Dundee for fresh, seasonal food and from the word go the café was incredibly popular. We're very proud that we've still got the same customers now as we did when we first opened (as well as quite a few more...).

The food we cook is mostly vegetarian, with meat and fish just used as an accent, thrown in to some sandwiches and tarts, but rarely the key ingredient. We buy everything we can locally, but our inspiration comes from further afield: the way people eat in the Middle East and southern Europe, mezze and tapas, a whole social, relaxed approach to food, with a strong vegetarian focus.

We run a pretty relaxed shop – Dundee is a very creative city and I think the café reflects that. With Duncan of Jordanstone College of Art & Design and the University of Dundee just around the corner, we have more than our share of artists and musicians and academics working in and eating at the café. I trained as an artist before cooking took over and the way our food looks has always been a big part of our ethos: it all looks really beautiful – jewel-like salads, golden pies, great slabs of cake. The café – those of you who are regulars will know – is tiny, but that hasn't stopped us doubling up as a gallery and a performance space to showcase the other creative lives of our staff. And the same sense of experimentation is on our menu; we've all really learned what we're doing on the job, and every day we try and take it a little bit further.

All these recipes are really easy, but they are aimed at people who love their food, and who aren't scared of hunting out slightly unusual ingredients. Increasingly you can get pretty much all of them at supermarkets, but I love the whole process of buying them in some of the small shops scattered about Dundee (and pretty much every other town in the UK): the Asian and Chinese supermarkets, Iranian corner shops, farmers markets and Polish grocers. It's always worth a poke about for an ingredient you're not entirely sure what to do with but you like the sound of.

The other thing about most of the recipes is that they'll show you a technique that you can then run with and add whatever flavours you like. That's how I learn, and how we cook in the café – I'll learn to make a specific thing in a specific way and then once I know how to do that I'll put my own twist on it. I hope that's something people can take from this book.

Enjoy.

Gillian Veal

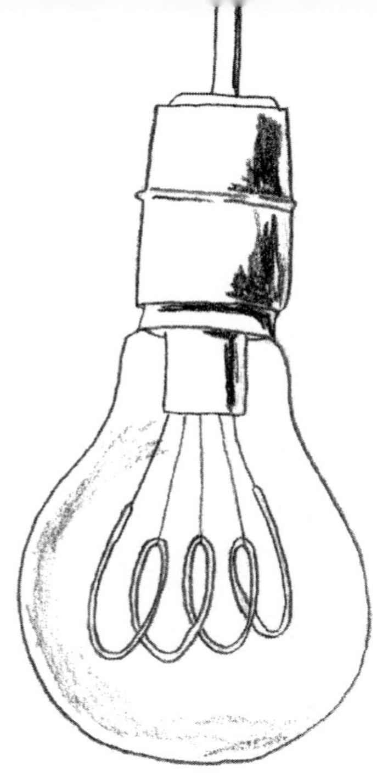

Note on Temperatures, Quantities & Measurements

Oven Temperatures

All temperatures in the recipes are for your bog standard electric oven. If you're cooking in a fan oven, you should lower the temperature by about 20C. If you've got a gas oven, check the chart below for conversions.

Gas Mark	C
1	140
2	150
3	170
4	180
5	190
6	200
7	220
8	230
9	240

Quantities & Measurements

An American cup measure is a handy thing to have, but if you've not got one, a cup is 250ml in a measuring jug (and a half cup, obviously, is 125ml).

Other useful conversions to know:

1 level teaspoon = 5ml

1 level tablespoon = 15ml

All eggs are large, and preferably free-range and organic, unless otherwise specified.

Most of the measurements in the recipes are precise and straightforward, but vegetables come in different shapes and sizes so often I have referred to, say, "a medium potato" or "a handful of flat leaf parsley". These are recipes where some flexibility is just fine, so go ahead and put in what you think is going to work. No catastrophes will happen if your potato is bigger than mine, and you'll end up making it according to your own taste, which is really what it's all about.

Breakfast, Brunch & Eggs

I love brunch in the café. I love weekends and I like the way the whole thing fits together – the customers come in more relaxed, we have the papers there for them, we really think about the music we put on for them and we make a little extra effort with their food.

We see brunch like this: if you're going to be 80% good and 20% bad then you'll be bad at weekends, and the brunch menu reflects that – it's time to treat yourself! So, when you're doing it at home, maybe getting together with friends, maybe just taking a bit more time to start your day well, remember the key things: simple, good ingredients, beautifully cooked. The best sausages and bacon you can get, free-range eggs at the very least, great bread, that sort of thing.

All these recipes make for a brilliant start to the day, but they're equally at home on the table for lunch, and really, brunch is more a frame of mind than an actual mealtime... so take your time and enjoy it.

Morning Glory Muffins

This is a great recipe. Alison from Yellow Door Bakery kindly shared this with me years ago, and it's incredibly easy and tasty and adaptable.

If you have more apples than carrots, just vary the proportions (making sure that the total is about 3 cups worth), and while walnuts and pecans seem to be the nuts that taste absolutely the best, I've also used almonds and they were delicious. You could substitute some toasted sunflower seeds as well. The batter is best prepared the day before you bake the muffins and will keep in the fridge for up to five days, so you could easily have a fresh muffin every weekday morning.

It really doesn't matter if you have an actual cup measurement; you can just use a measuring jug: 1 cup is equal to a 250ml measure, but to save you the maths I've given the metric conversion in brackets.

Ingredients

Group 1
1¼ cups sugar (310ml)
2 cups plain flour (500ml)
2 teaspoons cinnamon
2 teaspoons bicarbonate of soda
½ teaspoon salt

Group 2
½ cup shredded coconut (125ml)
½ cup raisins (125ml)
2 cups grated carrot (500ml)
1 cup grated apple (250ml)
½ cup roughly chopped nuts – either walnuts or pecans are best (125ml)

Group 3
3 eggs, lightly beaten
1 cup vegetable oil (250ml)
½ teaspoon vanilla extract

also...
12 muffin tins lined with paper cases

Mix all group 1 ingredients in one large bowl and the group 2 ingredients in another. Whisk everything in group 3 in a mixing jug.

Pour the contents of the jug into the bowl of group 1 ingredients and give it a quick stir to mix. Swiftly mix in the group 2 ingredients (the carrots etc.). Whenever you're making muffins, don't over mix the batter – it doesn't matter if there are small pockets of flour as it really will make the end result lighter. Put the batter in the fridge, covered, overnight.

The next morning, preheat the oven to 180C and spoon the batter into your waiting, lined muffin tins. Put in the oven until the muffins are golden, risen and springy to the touch – about 20 minutes.

Hot Potato and Chive Pancakes

A great dish to make for brunch, but equally as fine as a supper dish. These pancakes are a Parlour brunch staple, served with eggs and crispy smoked bacon or pan-fried garlicky mushrooms. They also go well with our tarragon sauce (see page 104).

In advance, bring the potatoes to the boil in salted water and, when cooked through and very tender, drain in a colander. Either mash them or put them through a potato ricer and set aside to cool down completely. In a large bowl beat the whole eggs and then mix thoroughly with the cooled potato. Stir in the flour.

Heat the milk to just under boiling and whisk into the potato and egg mixture. Add ½ a teaspoon of salt, a few grinds of black pepper and then the finely chopped chives. Whisk the egg whites until slightly stiff – no need to over do it, you just need to get some air in there. Add a third of the egg whites to the potato mixture to loosen it, and then gently fold in the rest. Taste a little of the mixture – it may need a touch more salt.

Heat a little oil in a very hot but not smoking non-stick pan and, using a tablespoon, drop in three little pancakes at a time. Cook for 2 to 3 minutes on each side until lightly browned, and serve hot.

Ingredients

500g floury potatoes
3 eggs and 2 egg whites
50g self raising flour
125ml milk
3 tablespoons finely chopped chives
sunflower oil
½ – 1 teaspoon salt
freshly ground black pepper

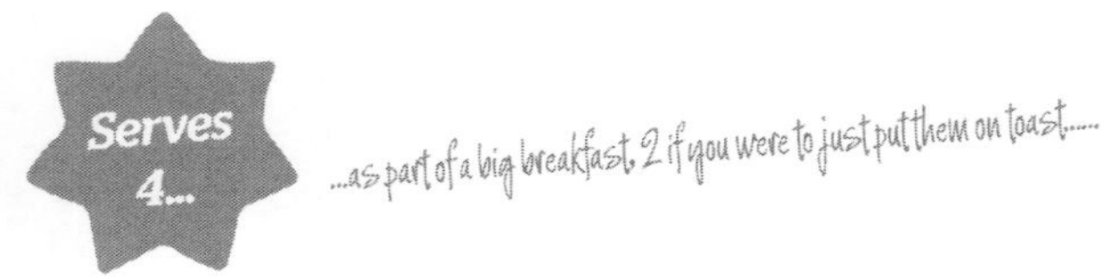

Perfect Breakfast Tomatoes

Very easy and very delicious.

Ingredients

4 ripe tomatoes, halved
2 sprigs thyme
1 clove garlic, crushed
100ml olive oil
1 teaspoon soft brown sugar
30ml balsamic vinegar
8 basil leaves
salt and freshly ground black pepper

Preheat the oven to 220C.

Put the halved tomatoes, cut side up, in a deep roasting tin. Put all the other ingredients in a jug and blitz with a hand blender, then pour over the tomatoes and bake for 20 minutes until bubbling and starting to brown.

That's it.

French Toast

A firm favourite in The Parlour. I don't think a day can go badly when you start with this, and kids love it. Top with whatever berries are in season, or banana and toffee or chocolate sauce, or savoury breakfast stuff such as sausage and bacon. You can use brioche instead of bread if you like but omit the vanilla essence if you do.

Break the eggs into a wide, shallow bowl and beat gently with the cream. If you're using them, add the cinnamon and/or nutmeg and the vanilla essence.

Over medium heat, heat a griddle or frying pan with a little butter or oil. Put the bread slices, one at a time, into the egg mixture and let them soak for a few seconds before carefully turning to coat the other side. Only soak the bread you will be cooking immediately or it turns to mush.

Fry the bread in the pan, leaving each piece until the bottom is crisp and golden brown before you flip it over and brown the other side. French toast is at its best hot with butter and syrup.

Ingredients

4 large eggs
50ml single cream
½ teaspoon cinnamon and/or a pinch of nutmeg (optional)
1 teaspoon vanilla essence
butter or oil for frying
8 thick slices white bread (preferably stale)
maple syrup

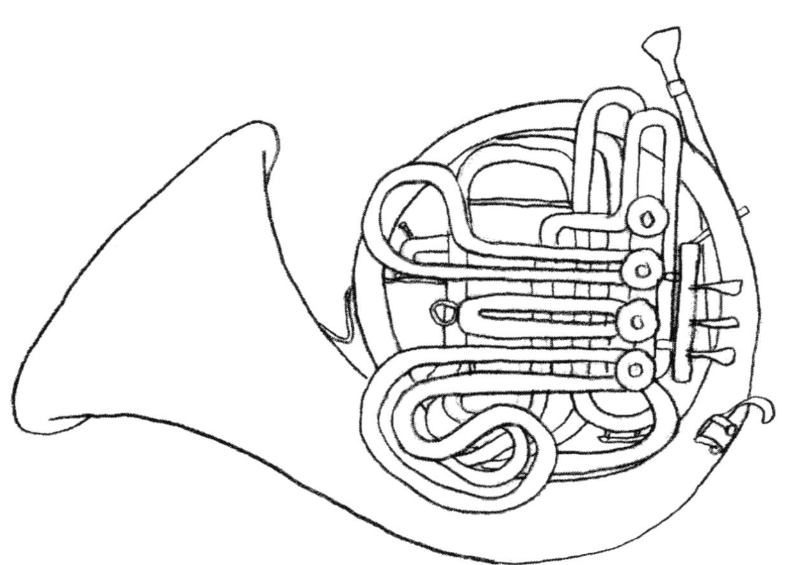

Oven Baked Mushroom and Cheddar Pancake

This is good made into a stack with crispy bacon and a fried egg.

Ingredients

1 tablespoon butter
1 tablespoon olive oil
1 onion, finely chopped
1 large clove garlic, crushed
225g chestnut mushrooms, chopped
1 tablespoon rosemary or thyme (or both), chopped
70g plain flour
2 eggs, beaten
225ml whole milk
1 tablespoon chives, finely chopped
1 tablespoon parsley, finely chopped
100g cheddar, grated
salt and freshly ground black pepper

Preheat the oven to 200C and put in a baking tray to heat up (not a cookie sheet – you need something with a rim). Put the butter and oil in a frying pan over a medium heat and let it get nice and hot before putting in the onions and garlic. Let them soften for 5 minutes (turning the heat down a tad to stop anything from burning) and then add the mushrooms and the rosemary or thyme and cook for a further 8 minutes until everything is soft and starting to turn golden brown.

Make the pancake batter by sifting the flour and a pinch of salt into a bowl. Mix the eggs, milk, chives and parsley in a jug and gradually stir into the flour to make a smooth batter. Season generously with freshly ground black pepper. Get your hot baking tray out of the oven, and spread the cooked mushroom mixture evenly over it. Gently pour over the pancake batter and then sprinkle with grated cheddar before returning to the oven and baking for 20 minutes. Cut into wedges and serve while still piping hot.

Sweet Potato, Roast Pepper and Feta Tortilla

Brilliant for brunch, but also great for a weekday lunch or supper. And it makes perfect picnic food.

Preheat the oven to 180C.

First roast the pepper – either put it in the oven until the skin is charred all over (about 45 minutes) or place under a hot grill and keep turning as the uppermost side blackens (which is quicker, but takes a bit more effort). Either way, once done, put the pepper in a bowl and cover with cling-film. When cool you should find the skin peels off easily, then remove the stalk and the seeds and cut the pepper into strips.

While the pepper is roasting, take the sweet potato and cut it into quarters lengthways before slicing across the way into thin slices about 3 – 5mm thick. Put the frying pan on a high heat and let it get really hot, and then add two tablespoons of olive oil and the sliced potato and chopped onion. Keep stirring until you get the heat through everything, then turn the heat to medium, cover and continue cooking, stirring every once in a while, until everything is soft. You may need to turn the heat down as the sweet potato cooks to stop it burning.

Beat the eggs with a good pinch of salt and some freshly ground black pepper in a large bowl. Add the hot potatoes and the leaves from one of the thyme sprigs and stir together gently. Meanwhile, wipe out the pan and put it back on a high heat with the remaining 3 tablespoons of oil. Once really hot, pour the potato, egg and thyme mixture back into the pan and give it a good shake to settle. Keep stirring with a flat edge wooden spatula from the middle out until the mix is almost cooked but still slightly runny.

Remove from the heat. Arrange the strips of roasted red pepper artfully over the tortilla, then crumble the feta and the leaves from the remaining sprig of thyme on top. Put the whole thing into the oven for 15 minutes or so – it's ready when it's all tinged with golden brown and is firm to the touch.

I like to serve this with a crisp green salad and Greek yoghurt and fresh mint on the side. Oh, and a squeeze of lemon.

Ingredients

1 red pepper
1 sweet potato, peeled
5 tablespoons olive oil
1 red onion, finely chopped
4 eggs
2 sprigs thyme leaves
100g feta cheese
salt and freshly ground black pepper

also...
You need an 8" frying pan, preferably non-stick, that can go into the oven.

Parma Baked Eggs

This may be the easiest recipe in the book but it's one of my favourites – fantastic as brunch, just as nice with some salad for lunch, or as a starter.

Preheat the oven to 180C.

Butter four ramekins and line them with two slices of Parma ham each, creating a little bowl. Crack an egg into each one and season with salt and pepper.

Bake in the oven for as long as it takes for the whites of the egg to set – about 20 minutes.

Ingredients

butter for greasing
8 slices Parma ham
4 eggs
salt and freshly ground black pepper

Crêpes

This recipe for crêpes is very versatile and great for using in main courses, brunch and pudding. I've given two savoury fillings here, but they are as good sweetened and eaten with lemon and sugar, or fresh fruit, or chocolate spread... Crêpes freeze brilliantly: just layer with greaseproof paper before you put in the freezer so you can take them out as you need them.

Ingredients

2 large eggs
140g plain flour
185ml milk
3 tablespoons melted butter
½ teaspoon salt
1 teaspoon of any finely chopped herbs (optional)
butter for frying

Whisk all the ingredients together in a large bowl and rest in the fridge for about an hour. Take it out and rest for another 15 minutes at room temperature.

Melt a small knob of butter in an 8 inch frying pan (preferably non-stick). Pour a ladleful of the mixture into the middle of the pan and then move and tilt the pan so the mixture coats the bottom evenly in a thin layer. Cook until the edges start to peel up (only 30 seconds or so), flip and cook for another 30 seconds – the crêpe should be lightly coloured.

Stack up on a plate before filling.

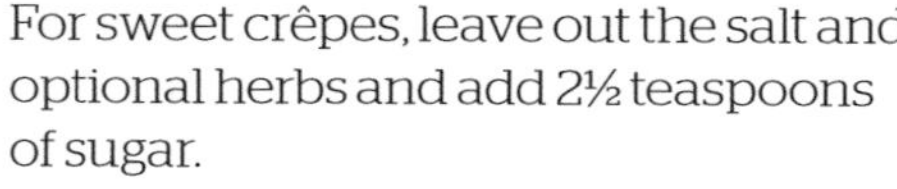

For sweet crêpes, leave out the salt and optional herbs and add 2½ teaspoons of sugar.

Two Savoury Fillings

Smoked Bacon, Caramelised Onion and Cheddar

8 rashers of trimmed smoked bacon, cooked til crisp and cut into strips
2 medium onions, sliced and slowly cooked until soft and sweet
200g strong cheddar, grated

Preheat the oven to 180C.

Simply scatter a strip of bacon, onion and cheese on each crêpe and roll them up. Line them all up in an oven dish and sprinkle more cheddar over the top, then bake until golden and bubbling – about 15 minutes.

Cream Cheese and Spicy Ratatouille

300g cream cheese
1 batch spicy ratatouille (see page 86)

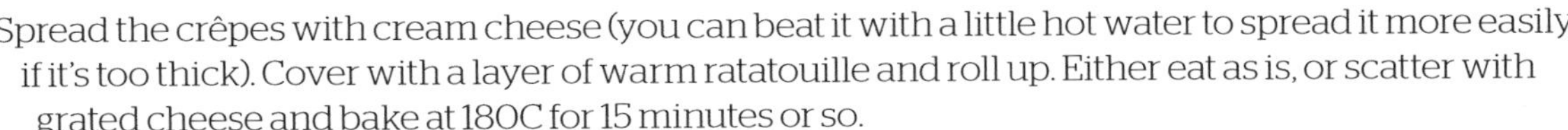

Spread the crêpes with cream cheese (you can beat it with a little hot water to spread it more easily if it's too thick). Cover with a layer of warm ratatouille and roll up. Either eat as is, or scatter with grated cheese and bake at 180C for 15 minutes or so.

Breads & Sandwiches

Making bread isn't something you can do in a hurry, but if you have a bit of time it's very easy and good fun. Freshly made flat-breads and coca bread are both great because once you've cracked the method, you can put anything you want on top. The breads here are all a cinch to make and don't need much in the way of kneading and proving, but they're also real crowd-pleasers and make your friends feel like you've made much more effort than you actually have – which is always good.

Whether your bread's home-made or a decent loaf from the shops, it usually ends up wrapped around some kind of a sandwich. We have a big take-away trade in the café, so sandwiches are a mainstay of what we do. Apart from using great bread and really classic flavour combinations, when we're making sandwiches we really try to make them appealing to the eye – bursting with texture and colour. Some of the ideas in this section are really simple – barely even a recipe – some a bit more complicated, but they're all heavy hitters when it comes to taste.

Coca Bread

This is a fantastic recipe from the Balearic Islands – a kind of Spanish pizza bread, but with a cakier, crumbier texture than normal pizza. Traditionally topped with peppers, onions and tomato, it works well with a variety of toppings (see below for some ideas) and is delicious hot or cold. It is also incredibly quick and easy to make as it doesn't need much in the way of kneading. Kids and adults love it!

Ingredients

1 teaspoon active dry yeast
250ml warmish water
500g plain flour
good pinch of salt
125ml olive oil

Preheat the oven to 180C.

Pour the yeast into the water in a measuring jug and stir in lightly with a fork so it starts to dissolve and froth. Put the flour and a pinch of salt into a large bowl and make an indentation in the middle, then pour the yeast-water mix and the olive oil into the hollow. Using two fingers, mix and stir from the middle out until the dough comes together. Give it a rough knead in the bowl to make sure it's all fully mixed – it will be soft and a bit sticky, but don't worry.

Cover the bowl with a damp tea towel and leave the dough to rise someplace warm. Grease a square or rectangular roasting dish with oil. After about an hour the dough should have doubled in size. Punch it down (literally, give it a punch in the middle), scoop up into a ball and press into your oiled roasting dish, making it higher at the edges. It doesn't really matter how thick the base is – in Spain it's always pretty thin, about 1cm, but I often make it thicker and cook it for a little longer.

Cover the dough surface with the topping of your choice (see topping suggestions below) and drizzle with a little olive oil.

Bake for approximately 25 to 30 minutes.

- ***Green pepper, onion and tomato – this is the most traditional one. Lightly sauté an onion with some garlic and sliced green pepper, add a chopped tomato and season with salt and freshly ground black pepper. Scatter on some olives once you've spread the vegetables on the dough.***
- ***A thin layer of spicy ratatouille (see page 86).***
- ***Roasted and peeled red peppers, maybe with some anchovies or salty cheese.***
- ***Our red onion marmalade (page 105), smeared thinly over the dough.***
- ***Cheese and ham – either keep it Spanish-style and use Manchego with Serrano ham, or go back to your roots and use strong cheddar and some shredded gammon.***

Rosemary and Anchovy Flat-Bread

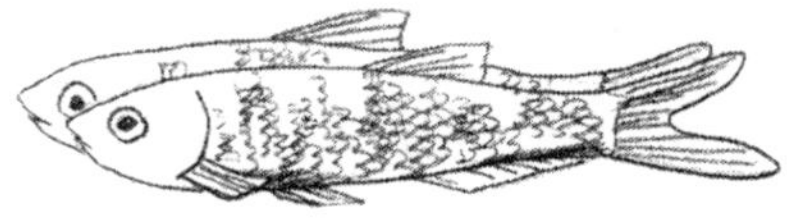

Ingredients

250g wholemeal flour
250g plain white flour
250ml warm water
½ teaspoon dried yeast
80ml olive oil
12 anchovy fillets
1 sprig of rosemary
salt and freshly ground black pepper

Mix both flours in a large bowl and make a well in the middle.

Dissolve the yeast in the warm water and gradually pour into the flour while mixing with the other hand. Pour in 60ml of the olive oil as well, and keep mixing until the ball of dough comes together. Turn the dough onto a lightly floured surface and knead until it becomes smooth and elastic – you will feel the dough changing and it will bounce back when you stick a finger into it (5 minutes should do it).

Cover the bowl with cling-film and set aside somewhere warm for about 1½ hours.

Meanwhile prepare the topping. Tear the leaves off the sprig of rosemary, chop them roughly and bash them up in a mortar and pestle with the anchovies and a glug or two of olive oil until you have a rough paste.

When the dough has about doubled in size, punch it down, gather into a ball and divide into 8 – 10 pieces depending on how many people you're feeding and how big you want your breads to be. Heat up the oven to 220C, and put in two lightly floured baking trays.

Roll the dough pieces out into rough circles, about half a centimetre thick, and evenly spread with the anchovy and rosemary paste. Push it into the dough with your fingers and make sure they're well covered.

Get the hot baking trays out of the oven, and place the waiting flat-breads on them. Sprinkle with sea salt, freshly ground black pepper and a drizzle of olive oil and put back in the oven for around 6 minutes until they are golden and starting to puff up.

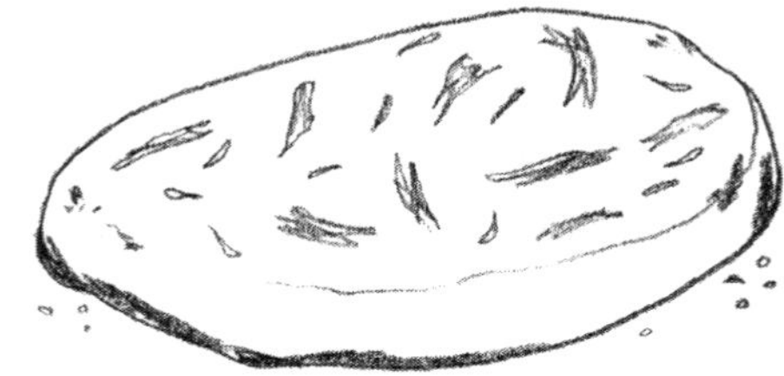

- *Chilli and garlic, mashed in a mortar and pestle with a few good glugs of olive oil.*
- *Pink peppercorn and rosemary – again, bash them up in a mortar and pestle with enough oil to make a paste.*

Three Recipes for Griddled Bread

Good bread, toasted and topped with juicy flavourful things – here are just three ideas.

All of them rely heavily on our own garlic butter (page 100) so make sure you have a batch of that at the ready.

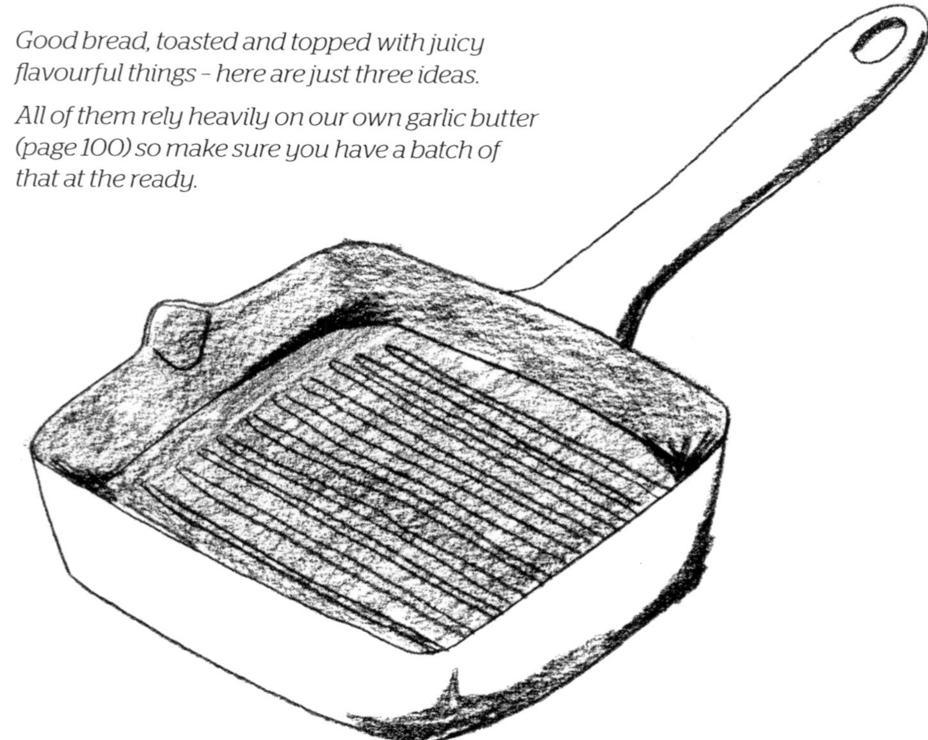

Chargrilled Halloumi, Roasted Vine Tomatoes and Sautéed Spinach

Preheat the oven to 220C.

Keeping the tomatoes on their vine, put them on a baking tray and drizzle with oil, then season with salt, pepper and the chopped chilli. Roast for about 10 to 15 minutes – until the skins are just starting to colour and burst. Turn the oven off.

Put a griddle pan on to get nice and hot. Brush the slices of halloumi with oil and griddle for 2 minutes on each side. While they're cooking, gently sweat the spinach in a tablespoon of the garlic butter in a medium saucepan. When they are cooked, put the tomatoes, cheese and spinach in the still-warm oven so they don't get cold. Now butter both sides of the bread with the remaining garlic butter and toast on the griddle pan for a couple of minutes each side.

Once the bread has crisped up nicely, evenly distribute the spinach on top of each slice, then put on a slice of halloumi and finally a sprig of roast tomatoes.

Serve with a simply dressed rocket salad.

Ingredients

4 sprigs cherry tomatoes on the vine
olive oil
1 small red chilli, deseeded and finely chopped
225g packet halloumi, sliced about 1cm thick
250g spinach
4 slices sourdough bread, cut about 2cm thick
3 tablespoons garlic butter (see page 100)
salt and freshly ground black pepper

Roasted Mushrooms with Taleggio and Thyme

Ingredients

24 closed cup mushrooms, wiped clean
1 tablespoon olive oil
4 tablespoons garlic butter (see page 100)
4 slices sourdough, cut about 2cm thick
250g taleggio cheese
4 sprigs thyme
salt and freshly ground black pepper

Preheat the oven to 220C.

Put the mushrooms on a baking tray, drizzle with oil and smear two tablespoons of the garlic butter over them. Scatter the thyme leaves all over and season generously, then roast for around 15 minutes. While they're cooking, spread both sides of the bread with the remaining garlic butter and heat up the griddle pan so it's nice and hot. Griddle the bread for 2 minutes on each side and place on a baking tray.

Divide the roasted mushrooms between the griddled bread slices and roughly break the taleggio over the top.

Return to the oven for 5 to 8 minutes until the cheese is melting and starting to bubble and then eat it up, straight away.

Parmesan-Crusted Aubergine, Chorizo and Rocket with Roasted Garlic Aioli

This might look complicated for what is essentially an open sandwich, but it really is worth it. The parmesan-crusted aubergine also makes a great starter or side dish on its own.

Preheat the oven to 220C.

Put the chorizos, whole, on a baking tray in the oven and roast for 12 minutes until they're starting to brown up. Slice lengthways and leave to cool on a plate. Turn the oven off. Chop the aubergine in half widthways, then cut each half lengthways into slices about 1cm thick. Mix the breadcrumbs, parmesan and rosemary together and put on a plate, then put the beaten eggs into a shallow bowl, and the flour, seasoned with salt and pepper, on another plate. Have another large plate or baking tray on standby.

Now, crust your aubergine! Dip each slice in the seasoned flour, then in the beaten egg, and finally in the cheesy, herby breadcrumbs. Make sure the slices are well covered in crumbs and put on the baking tray or plate you have waiting. Once they are all coated, pour oil into a large frying pan to about 1cm deep and put over a medium heat. When the oil is hot, shallow fry the aubergine on both sides until crispy and golden. Put the cooked slices on kitchen paper on a plate and put in the cooling-down oven to keep warm.

Put the griddle pan on a medium high heat and, while it's getting nice and hot, spread both sides of the bread slices with plenty of garlic butter. Griddle on both sides for about 2 minutes.

To assemble, top each slice of griddled bread with a handful of fresh rocket, then slices of chorizo, then the golden-crumbed aubergine and finally a big old spoon of garlic aioli on the very top.

Ingredients

4 cooking chorizos
(we use the small Brindisa ones)
1 aubergine
100g fresh breadcrumbs
100g parmesan, finely grated
1 sprig rosemary, finely chopped
2 eggs, beaten
3 heaped tablespoons plain flour
sunflower oil for shallow frying
4 slices sourdough, sliced about 2cm thick
2 tablespoons garlic butter
(see page 100)
4 tablespoons roasted garlic aioli
(see page 96)
4 handfuls rocket
salt and freshly ground black pepper

Chorizo, Rocket and Roasted Garlic Aioli Rolls

I first came across this at a stall on Borough Market in London; there is always a massive queue for this simple but super tasty sandwich. It's worth saving the oil that's rendered when you fry the chorizo: it's very delicious and good to add to soups or mayonnaise or to drizzle over eggs.

Ingredients

8 good quality cooking chorizos (we use Brindisa)
4 rustic bread rolls (something like foccacia or sourdough)
100g rocket
4 tablespoons roasted garlic aioli (see page 96)
1 lemon, quartered
salt and freshly ground black pepper

Cut the chorizos in half lengthways and cook on a griddle for about 8 minutes. Chorizo releases a lot of oil when it cooks so you shouldn't need to add any.

Warm the rolls in the oven, then split and simply assemble the sandwich in this order: rocket, chorizo, aioli, squeeze of lemon and finally salt and pepper.

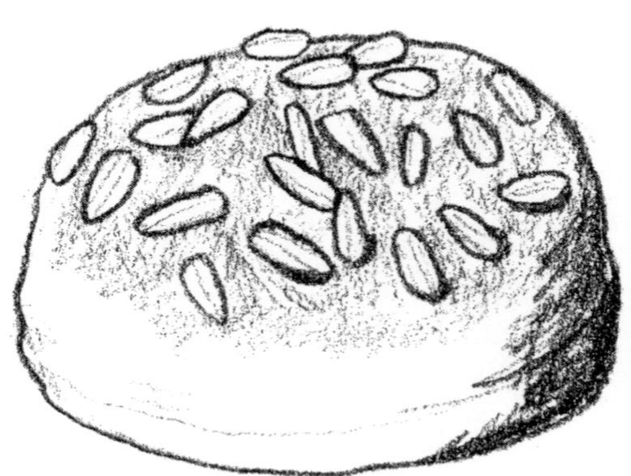

Pastrami, Brie and Red Onion Marmalade Bagel

Gillian Martin (one of the first chefs to work with me at The Parlour) created this sandwich years ago and it's been on the menu ever since. It is by far our most popular sandwich. You can get pastrami from any decent butcher, or indeed, at the supermarket.

Preheat the oven to 200C.

Cut the bagels open and place on a baking tray, cut side up. On the bottom half of each bagel, place 2 radicchio leaves, 2 slices of pastrami, a slice of brie and a tablespoon of red onion marmalade.

Bake in the oven for 5 minutes, then replace the top halves and serve hot, with a gherkin.

Ingredients

4 bagels
8 radicchio leaves
8 slices peppered pastrami
4 slices brie, about 5mm thick
4 tablespoons red onion marmalade (see page 105)
4 gherkins

Goats Cheese Bruschetta Two Ways

Goats Cheese and Red Onion Marmalade with Pine Nuts and Thyme

Preheat the oven to 200C.

Simple: spread the toasted bread with red onion marmalade, then lay on a slice of goats cheese, sprinkle with pine nuts and put on a baking tray in the oven until the goats cheese and pine nuts start to colour. Serve with a simple green salad and balsamic dressing.

Ingredients

4 slices toasted bread, about 2cm thick

4 tablespoons red onion marmalade (see page 105)

4 slices chevre goats cheese, about 1cm thick

4 teaspoons pine nuts

Goats Cheese, Pistachios, Honey and Rosewater

This is lovely served with a bitter leaf salad (endive or chicory is good) and our orange, honey and sesame salad dressing.

Preheat the oven to 200C.

Put the pistachios on a baking tray and roast in the oven for 5 minutes. Put in a mortar and pestle with two tablespoons of honey and the rosewater and pound into a rough paste. Lay a slice of goats cheese on each piece of toast, then spread with the pistachio paste and drizzle the whole thing with a bit more honey.

Put on a baking tray in the oven and bake for 5 to 10 minutes, watching carefully that the topping doesn't burn.

Ingredients

4 tablespoons unsalted pistachios, shelled

3 tablespoons runny honey

1½ teaspoons rosewater

4 slices chevre goats cheese, about 1cm thick

4 slices toasted bread, about 2cm thick

Pan Bagnat

This is a great sandwich to take on a picnic. If you are feeling decadent, by all means use fresh tuna that you have cooked and flaked, but we use good quality tinned.

Ingredients

1 large ciabatta
3 boiled eggs, peeled and sliced
370g tuna (i.e. 2 tins, drained)
180g black olives, pitted and chopped
8 anchovies, chopped (optional)
1 sweet red pepper, finely chopped
3 ripe tomatoes, finely chopped
1 red onion, finely chopped
1 small garlic clove, crushed
1 heaped teaspoon dried oregano
125ml salsa verde (see page 97)
2 tablespoons olive oil
juice of ½ a lemon
salt and freshly ground black pepper

Take the ciabatta and slice it in half lengthways. Take out most of the bread from the middle, and discard (or use to make breadcrumbs), leaving a sturdy shell around the edges.

Put all the remaining ingredients in a large bowl and use your hands to mush it together, really blending all the flavours. Pack this into the bottom half of the ciabatta, then put the top half back on and wrap the whole thing tightly in cling-film. Now put it between 2 chopping boards and put a weight on top (4 tins of tomatoes should do the trick). Leave it for at least 4 hours, preferably overnight.

When you're ready to eat, unwrap, cut into fat slices and eat.

Beware, it can be messy!

Croque Monsieur with Mushrooms

This is the Parlour version of the French traditional sandwich, great for brunch or weekday lunch. Leave out the ham and add more mushrooms to make it veggie, or indeed leave out the mushrooms and you've got the classic Croque Monsieur.

Get a frying pan nice and hot and lightly fry the mushrooms in a tablespoon of the oil, crumbling in the thyme whilst they are cooking. Season lightly with salt and pepper and set them aside. Stir the mustard into the béchamel sauce.

Butter four slices of bread, and scatter half of the grated emmental over them. Cover the cheese with a slice of ham, and on top of that spread a tablespoon of béchamel sauce. Scatter with a few of the cooked mushrooms, and place a second piece of bread on top.

Heat the remaining tablespoon of oil in a large frying pan and when it's hot, put in the sandwiches, right side up, for a few minutes – just to get the underside crispy. Then carefully transfer the sandwiches to a baking tray, still right side up.

Spread the top of each sandwich with a heaped tablespoon of béchamel sauce (if it drizzles down the edges, so much the better) then scatter with the remaining cheese. Place under a medium grill until everything is brown and bubbly and eat immediately whilst piping hot.

Ingredients

2 field mushrooms, sliced
2 tablespoons olive oil
1 teaspoon fresh thyme
2 teaspoons Dijon mustard
1 quantity béchamel sauce (see page 103) – you'll have some left over but you can use that for cauliflower cheese, or a vegetable gratin
8 thick slices good white bread
butter (at room temperature)
200g emmental cheese, grated
4 slices good quality ham or left-over roast gammon
salt and freshly ground black pepper

Soups

You know, you can't go wrong with soup. If you're pushed for time or just want to do something on the cheap, you can happily feed your family or a group of friends with one big pot and a loaf of bread. We sell 20 to 30 litres of it a day, winter and summer, and these are the recipes for some of our most popular ones. You can go a long way with a hand blender, some vegetables and a load of fresh herbs – that's all you really need to know.

Carrot, Cumin and Coconut Soup

Ingredients

2 tablespoons sesame oil
1 large red onion, finely sliced
2 garlic cloves, finely chopped
1 red chilli, finely chopped
1 teaspoon fennel seeds
1½ teaspoons cumin seeds
2 teaspoons root ginger, peeled and finely chopped
750g carrots, peeled and chopped
½ teaspoon turmeric
200ml coconut milk (½ a tin)
½ – 1 teaspoon bouillon powder to taste
salt and freshly ground black pepper

Heat the sesame oil in a large saucepan and cook the onion over a medium high heat until it starts to brown lightly at the edges. Turn down the heat a little and add the garlic, chilli, fennel, cumin and ginger. Fry, stirring, for a couple of minutes until the smell rises from the spices.

Add the carrots, stir well, and leave to cook with the lid on for 5 minutes or so before sprinkling over the turmeric. Pour in enough water to just cover the carrots, bring to the boil and then simmer, covered, for about 30 minutes. Once the carrots are very tender, pour in the coconut milk and liquidise til silky smooth (you may need to do this in batches). Season with bouillon powder to taste and then again with salt and freshly ground black pepper.

Squash, Apple and Ginger Soup

Melt the butter in a large saucepan and add the onion and garlic, frying them until they are soft and translucent.

Add the allspice and ginger and fry for another couple of minutes, then throw in the squash and apple and cook for about 10 minutes or until the squash starts to caramelise at the edges.

Pour in the stock, bring to the boil and simmer until the squash is absolutely soft – about 20 minutes should do it. Blitz with your hand blender until smooth, and season with salt and freshly ground pepper.

Ingredients

20g butter
1 large onion, finely chopped
2 cloves garlic, crushed
½ teaspoon allspice
2 inch piece of ginger, finely grated
1 butternut squash, peeled, de-seeded, and cut into 1cm dice
3 apples, peeled, cored and roughly chopped
1.5l vegetable stock
salt and freshly ground pepper (pink peppercorns work particularly well)

Mediterranean Vegetable Soup

Ingredients

2 tablespoons olive oil
1 large onion, chopped
1 large leek, washed and chopped
1 large carrot, chopped
1 fennel bulb, chopped
1 large sprig of rosemary
6 garlic cloves, finely chopped
1 red chilli, finely chopped
1 sweet potato, cut into 1cm dice
600g tomatoes, roughly chopped
200g cooked cannellini beans (½ a 400g tin)
½ – 1 teaspoon vegetable bouillon powder
200g broccoli, chopped into florets
1 large handful green beans, chopped into 3cm lengths
3 tablespoons pesto
salt and freshly ground black pepper

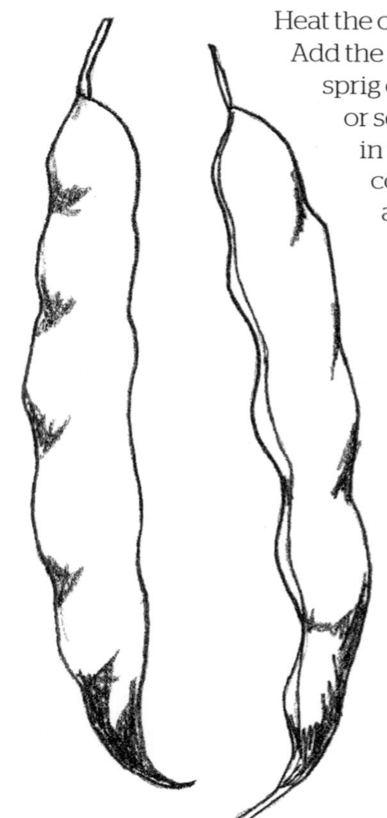

Heat the olive oil in a large saucepan over a medium heat. Add the onion, leek, carrot and fennel along with the sprig of rosemary. Sweat with a lid on for 10 minutes or so, until the veg is soft and starting to colour. Stir in the garlic, chilli, sweet potato and tomatoes and cook uncovered for another 10 minutes, before adding the cannellini beans. Give it all a good stir and just cover with water. Sprinkle on a little bouillon, but go carefully as the pesto will also bring flavour later. Bring to the boil and simmer, half covered, for 15 minutes.

Meanwhile, boil a pan of water and cook the broccoli and green beans for a few minutes until just tender. Add to the soup with the pesto, and season to taste with a touch more bouillon, salt and plenty of freshly ground black pepper.

Tomato and Mint Soup

Simple and delicious, and it freezes brilliantly. If the tomato stalks are removed before cooking then it is not as necessary to strain the soup through the sieve. The soup will of course not be as smooth, but it will still be tasty!

Ingredients

60g unsalted butter
2 medium onions, roughly chopped
1.25kg vine tomatoes, stalks and all
½ tablespoon sugar
110ml sherry
10g (large handful) fresh mint, chopped
salt and freshly ground black pepper

Melt the butter in a large saucepan, then stir in the onions and cook on a medium high heat until they are soft and golden in colour. Add the tomatoes, sugar and sherry to the pan, bring to the boil then cover and simmer on a low heat for around an hour.

Blend in a food processor until smooth (you may need to do this in batches), then strain the soup through a sieve into a clean pan, helping it on its way by pushing through with a metal spoon.

Stir in the chopped mint and season to taste.

Easy!

Cannellini Bean, Garlic and Sage Soup

Preheat the oven to 220C.

Slice the very top off the garlic bulb horizontally so you can see into all the cloves, then wrap it loosely in tin foil and roast in the oven for 30 minutes, until soft and golden. Leave to get cool.

Meanwhile, heat the olive oil in your big soup pot and cook the remaining, unroasted garlic cloves and onion until translucent. Splash in the white wine and carry on cooking until all the liquid has evaporated, then add the stock and the beans and simmer, half covered, until the beans are soft enough to squash with a spoon. (Depending on the age of the beans this can take anything from 40 minutes to 2 hours.) Squeeze in the soft insides of the roasted garlic (easy, because you sliced the tops off the cloves earlier), add the sage and simmer for another 10 minutes.

Roughly blend or mash the soup (you want a bit of texture) and season with salt and plenty of freshly ground black pepper.

Ingredients

1 whole garlic bulb
3 tablespoons olive oil
4 cloves garlic, finely chopped
1 large white Spanish onion, finely chopped
½ glass white wine
1.5l vegetable stock
300g dried cannellini beans, soaked overnight
4 sprigs sage, finely chopped
salt and freshly ground black pepper

Roasted Carrot, Pepper and Smoked Paprika Soup

Ingredients

2 small red peppers
6 medium carrots
2 sprigs thyme, destalked
2 tablespoons olive oil
1 large onion, chopped
2 cloves garlic, chopped
1 teaspoon smoked paprika
1l vegetable stock
salt and freshly ground black pepper

Preheat the oven to 200C.

Roughly chop the peppers and carrots and put on a large baking tray (you may need a couple). Sprinkle with the thyme and drizzle with a tablespoon of the oil, using your hands to make sure all the vegetables are coated, then roast for 15 minutes until the edges are just starting to turn golden.

Meanwhile, heat the remainder of the oil in a large soup pot and soften the onions and garlic over a medium low heat. Add the peppers and carrots and cook for a further 5 minutes before sprinkling on the paprika. Stir and cook for a minute or so, add the stock and bring to the boil, then reduce the heat and simmer for 25 minutes. Using a hand blender, purée the soup til smooth and thick.

Delicious as is, even better with a dollop of crème fraiche and a grating of lime in each bowl.

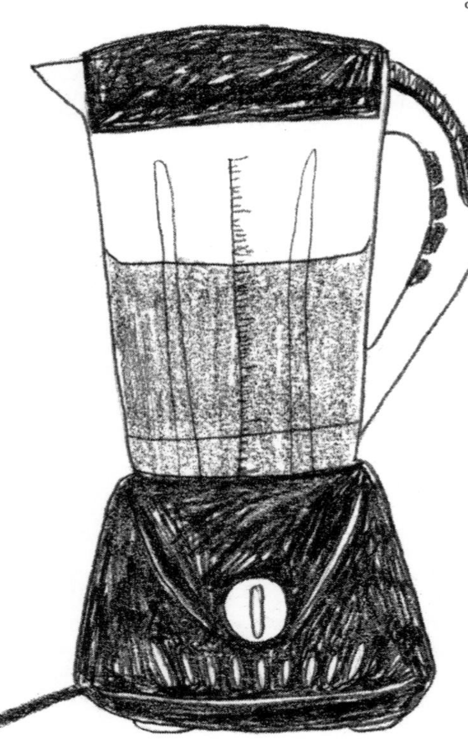

Butter Bean, Carrot and Rosemary Soup

This is a great standby soup – you can use tinned butter beans if you're pushed for time, and it freezes beautifully. So if you're feeling domestic and efficient, double up the recipe and freeze half for another time. It's also good with some finely chopped sausage or bacon added at the same time as the carrots.

If you're starting from scratch with the butter beans, put the soaked beans in a large pot and generously cover them with water. Bring to the boil and simmer until very soft (this can take up to 1½ hours depending on the age of the beans).

Put the oil in your soup pot over a medium heat. Once hot, stir in the onion and garlic and cook until they begin to soften. Then add the chopped carrots and continue cooking until they begin to caramelise – keep stirring and if the carrots and onions start to catch or burn, add a splash of water and turn the heat down a little. After about 20 minutes the vegetables should be soft, sweet and golden. Turn the heat up a bit and pour in the wine and the chopped rosemary, bringing it to the boil and bubbling away until the wine has almost completely evaporated. Keep stirring from time to time to stop it catching on the bottom of the pan.

Add the stock, the cooked and drained butter beans and the parsley and simmer for 10 to 15 minutes. Liquidise until smooth, and season with salt and plenty of freshly ground black pepper.

Ingredients

500g butter beans soaked overnight (or 2 tins, drained)
2 tablespoons olive oil
1 large onion, chopped
4 cloves garlic, finely chopped
500g carrots, chopped
100ml white wine
1 large sprig rosemary, finely chopped
1.5l stock, vegetable or chicken both work fine
small bunch flat leaf parsley, roughly chopped
salt and freshly ground black pepper

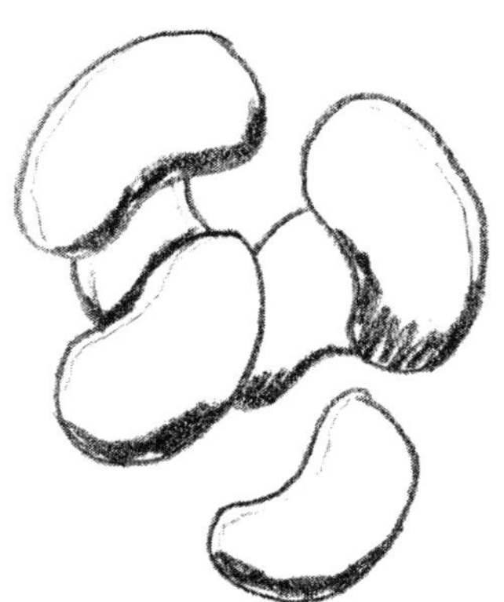

Parlour Minestrone

A great soup for using up all the odds and ends of vegetables you have lying about – feel free to put in whatever's handy.

Ingredients

3 tablespoons olive oil
1 large onion, chopped
3 cloves garlic, finely chopped
2 medium carrots, chopped
2 tablespoons tomato purée
1 sprig thyme
400g tin chopped tomatoes (or 6 fresh ones, skinned and chopped)
1 aubergine, cut into 1cm cubes
1 large potato, peeled and cut into 1cm cubes
1.2l vegetable stock
150g peas (fresh or frozen)
150g French beans, chopped into 2cm lengths
1 medium courgette, cut into 1cm cubes
400g tin cannellini beans
100g orzo pasta
75g parmesan
salt and freshly ground black pepper

Put your soup pot over a medium heat and pour in the oil. Once it's hot, add the onions and garlic and fry until they are soft and translucent. Then stir in the carrots, tomato purée and thyme leaves and sweat for 10 minutes with the lid on.

Put in the tomatoes and aubergine and cook for a further 5 minutes before adding the potatoes and stock. Leave to simmer for 10 minutes, until the potatoes are nearly tender, then put in the peas, French beans, courgette and beans. Bring back up to the boil, scatter in the orzo, give the whole lot a good stir and simmer for a final 10 minutes – by which time the vegetables should all be tender but not falling to pieces and the pasta will be al dente.

Just before serving, grate the parmesan into the soup and season with a little salt and plenty of freshly ground black pepper.

Roasted Beetroot and Garlic Soup

Preheat the oven to 220C.

Wrap all the beetroot and the cloves of garlic in a big tin foil parcel and roast for an hour or so, until the beetroot are tender and a knife goes easily into them. Leave to cool, then peel and chop the lot. In your soup pot, heat the oil and add the onion and celery, cooking until soft and transparent. Stir in the roasted beetroot, garlic and chopped rosemary, then pour in the stock and simmer for 20 minutes. Blitz until smooth with a hand blender and stir in the balsamic vinegar. Season with salt and lots of freshly ground black pepper to taste.

Serve with a swirled teaspoon of soured cream and a sprinkling of lemon zest in each bowl.

Ingredients

550g beetroot
6 garlic cloves
2 tablespoons olive oil
1 large onion, finely chopped
1 stick celery, finely chopped
½ teaspoon rosemary, finely chopped
750ml vegetable stock
2 tablespoons balsamic vinegar
4 teaspoons soured cream
zest of 1 unwaxed lemon
salt and freshly ground black pepper

Spinach, Courgette and Parmesan Soup

Easy, and very good.

Ingredients

2 tablespoons olive oil
2 garlic cloves, finely chopped
1 onion, finely chopped
2 courgettes, grated
2 medium potatoes, peeled and diced (mine weighed about 300g)
750ml vegetable stock
100g baby spinach
50g parmesan, grated
salt and freshly ground black pepper

Heat the oil in the soup pot and gently fry the garlic and onion until soft and transparent. Stir in the courgette and cook for a further 5 minutes, then add the potatoes and stock and simmer until everything is tender (20 minutes or so). Put in the spinach and simmer again until it's fully wilted, then blitz until smooth with a hand blender, season to taste and stir in the grated parmesan to serve.

Red Lentil and Lemon Soup

This is a classic soup from the Middle East, strangely reassuring and reviving.

Heat the olive oil in your big soup pot, then add the onion and garlic and cook until the onions begin to soften. Stir in the carrot, tomato purée, ground cumin and cayenne pepper and cook for another 15 minutes. When everything is soft and golden, pour in the stock and the lentils.

Bring to the boil and simmer, covered, for 30 minutes or until the lentils have started to fall apart. Add the lemon juice and zest and season with the nutmeg, ½ a teaspoon of salt and plenty of freshly ground black pepper. Blitz with a hand blender until smooth and serve.

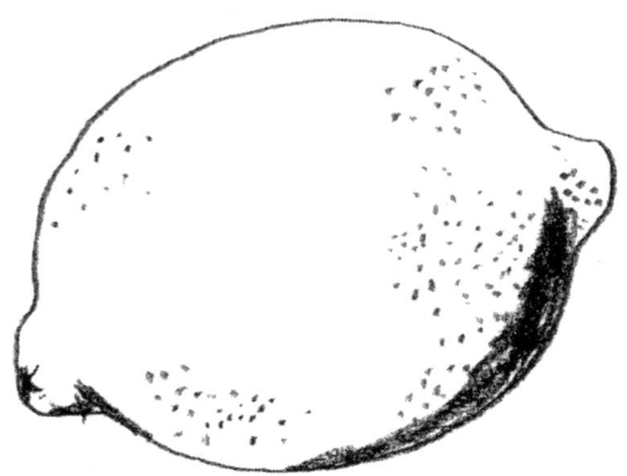

Ingredients

2 tablespoons olive oil
1 large white Spanish onion, chopped
2 garlic cloves, grated
1 large carrot, peeled and chopped
1½ tablespoons tomato purée
½ tablespoon cumin seeds, toasted and ground
1 pinch cayenne pepper
1l vegetable stock
200g red lentils, rinsed
zest and juice of 1 unwaxed lemon
¼ teaspoon nutmeg, grated
salt and freshly ground black pepper

Salads & Mezze

Salads have been the big success story of The Parlour – we didn't start out having a salad bar but they just crept on and on until they became our trademark. I love making them: they're simple, colourful, healthy and most of all really, really tasty. They also give me an opportunity to use more unusual ingredients like orzo or quinoa, and I've been constantly amazed by people who've been willing to try new things. We get big blokes coming in to the café who have probably been told to start eating something healthy by their wives, so they eat one of our salads and the next thing you know they're back saying 'I don't know what that is, but I'll have it again please' because they loved the way it tasted. That's a real victory for me. The dressings are crucial as that's what will really make a salad sing, and the rest of it is all about putting together unusual combinations, trying flavours out and getting surprised by the outcomes.

Aubergine, Walnut and Mint Dip

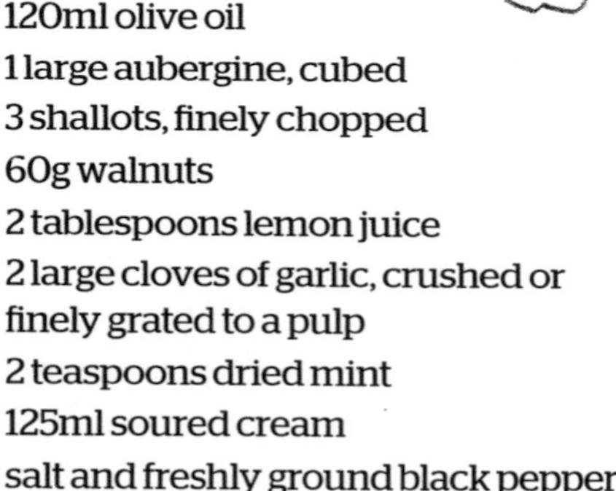

Ingredients

120ml olive oil
1 large aubergine, cubed
3 shallots, finely chopped
60g walnuts
2 tablespoons lemon juice
2 large cloves of garlic, crushed or finely grated to a pulp
2 teaspoons dried mint
125ml soured cream
salt and freshly ground black pepper

Heat a large frying pan with about 90ml of the oil and fry the aubergine over a medium heat til golden and soft. Turn the heat down slightly, add the shallots and cook for a further 2 minutes.

While the aubergines are cooking, lightly toast the walnuts in a dry frying pan. Using a food processor or hand blender, blend the aubergine mixture with the lemon juice, garlic and walnuts until smooth, adding a a little extra olive oil if it needs loosening up. Season with salt and pepper to taste. In a small bowl, mix the dried mint with 2 tablespoons of olive oil. Spread the aubergine puree on a plate, top with soured cream and then drizzle over the minty oil.

Serve at room temperature with warm flat-breads for scooping.

Tomato, Chilli, Coriander and Garlic Dip

This is delicious with fresh, warm flat-breads and pan-fried halloumi, or as part of a mezze table. Fresh tomatoes are best when they are sweet and in season – if not use a tin and a half of plum tomatoes, drained, and add a level tablespoon of sugar.

To skin the tomatoes, slash them with a knife and drop into a bowl of just boiled water. Leave for 10 seconds, and when you pull them out the skin will have started to curl up at the edges. Peel it off and chop the tomatoes.

Blitz the chilli, garlic and coriander in a blender to a rough paste. Heat up the oil in a frying pan and sauté the paste for a couple of minutes. Add the tomatoes, stir and simmer over a low heat for about 20 minutes, then cover and cook for a further 5 minutes until you've got a jammy texture. Season with salt and pepper and leave to cool before serving.

Ingredients

6 tomatoes
3 tablespoons olive oil
1 red chilli, deseeded and chopped (leave the seeds in if you like it hot)
5 garlic cloves
1 small bunch coriander, roughly chopped
3 tablespoons olive oil
salt and freshly ground black pepper

Red Pepper Tapenade

Amazing to use on bruschetta or as a dip. Despite the long list of ingredients, this is really easy to make.

Ingredients

2 medium sweet red peppers, chopped
1 small onion, chopped
1 large or 2 small red chillis (deseed if you don't like it too hot)
1 sprig rosemary, finely chopped
5 large garlic cloves
2 tablespoons olive oil
75g blanched almonds
a good pinch of cumin seeds
½ teaspoon coriander seeds, roasted and crushed
1 handful coriander, finely chopped
salt and freshly ground black pepper

Preheat the oven to 180C.

Place the sweet peppers, onion, chilli, rosemary and 3 cloves of the garlic, finely chopped, on a baking tray and season. Drizzle with a tablespoon of the olive oil. Put in the oven and bake for around 15 minutes until the vegetables are starting to soften.

Put the almonds on another tray and put them in the oven at the same time to roast – keep an eye on them as they burn quickly. Then chuck the contents of both trays in a food processor and blitz until smooth. Leave to cool in a bowl, then add the rest of the olive oil, cumin and coriander seeds, the two remaining cloves of garlic, crushed, and the fresh coriander, stirring well to mix. Season if you think it needs it and that's it.

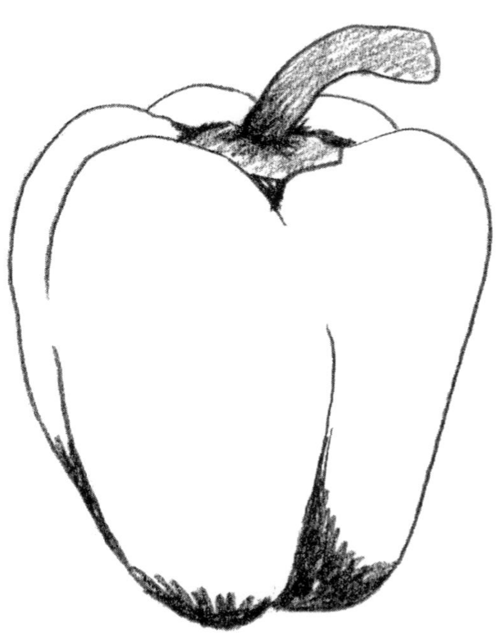

Beetroot, Quinoa, Feta and Orange Salad

This salad is brilliant. It looks beautiful, it's easy to make, it's really good for you and it's super tasty. I could keep adding ingredients to this but the simplicity is what I like about it. I love it on its own, but it also makes a good stuffing for peppers or tomatoes and is great with a roast.

Ingredients

1½ cups (375ml in a measuring jug) quinoa
2 raw beetroot, grated
2 oranges, zested then peeled and sliced
generous handful of baby spinach, shredded
2 tablespoons fresh mint, finely chopped
1 red chilli, finely chopped
4 tablespoons balsamic, honey and mustard dressing (see page 94)
250g feta cheese
1 lemon, cut into 6 wedges
salt and freshly ground black pepper

To cook the quinoa, bring a pan of salted water to the boil and then add the grains. I cook it for 12 minutes or so, until the grains are tender and you see the little tails come out. Then rinse in cold water and leave to dry in a sieve.

Once dry, put the quinoa in a serving bowl with the beetroot, orange zest and slices, the spinach, mint and chilli, then stir in the balsamic dressing. Keep folding gently until the grains have turned a deep pink.

Just before serving, crumble the feta through the salad, add salt and pepper to taste (the amount of salt you need will depend on the saltiness of your feta) and serve with a wedge of lemon.

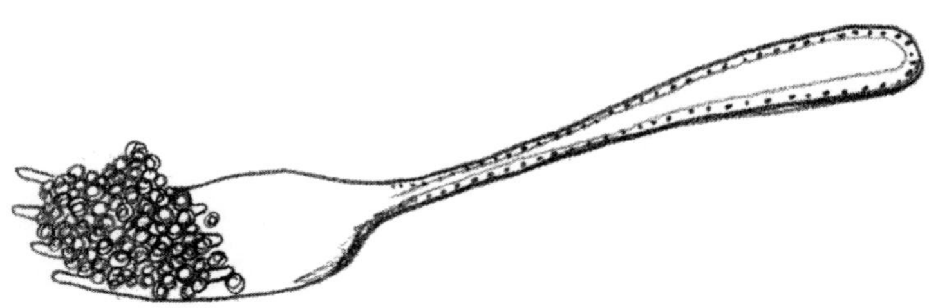

Puy Lentil and Goats Cheese Salad

Cook the lentils in boiling water for 20 minutes, until they are absolutely tender. Meanwhile, fry the onion, carrot, celery, thyme and the bay leaf in a couple of tablespoons of the olive oil until soft and lightly coloured. In a food processor or with a hand blender, blend the garlic with the rest of the olive oil. With the motor still running, slowly pour in the vinegar and blend until it's emulsified.

Drain the lentils and pour out onto a flattish dish. Smother in the garlicky dressing and turn gently so everything is glistening. Once the vegetables are cooked, gently mix them into the lentils and leave the salad to cool. Then toss gently with the goats cheese, torn into chunks, and the parsley. Season with salt and freshly ground pepper if you think it needs it.

Ingredients

200g Puy lentils
1 onion, chopped
1 carrot, chopped
2 stalks celery, chopped
4 sprigs fresh thyme
1 bay leaf
150ml extra virgin olive oil
3 – 6 garlic cloves, peeled and roughly chopped (I use 6, but it all depends how feisty you like it...)
50ml red wine vinegar
100g goats cheese
large handful parsley, roughly chopped
salt and freshly ground black pepper

Cannellini Bean, Baby Spinach and Roasted Red Pepper Salad

This is a really good salad to have with some left-over weekend roast meat.

Ingredients

1 red pepper
1 small red onion
5 tablespoons white wine vinegar
400g tin cannellini beans, drained and rinsed
200g spinach, washed and shredded
½ tablespoon honey
1½ tablespoons lemon juice
2 tablespoons olive oil
½ teaspoon Dijon mustard
¼ teaspoon chilli flakes
salt and freshly ground black pepper

First roast the pepper – either put it in the oven until the skin is charred all over (about 45 minutes), or place under a hot grill and keep turning as the uppermost sides blacken (which is quicker, but takes a bit more effort). Either way, once done, put the pepper in a bowl and cover with clingfilm. When cool, peel off the skin, then remove the stalk and the seeds and tear the flesh into strips.

While the pepper is roasting, slice the red onion thinly and put in a small bowl with the white wine vinegar. Leave to marinate for 30 minutes, then remove the onions and save the vinegar for the dressing.

Put the marinated onions, cannellini beans, roasted pepper strips and shredded spinach in a large salad bowl. Then make the dressing: whisk together the honey, lemon juice, olive oil and mustard with 1 tablespoon of the vinegar from the onions. Add the chilli flakes and season to taste, then pour over the salad and toss gently until everything is covered.

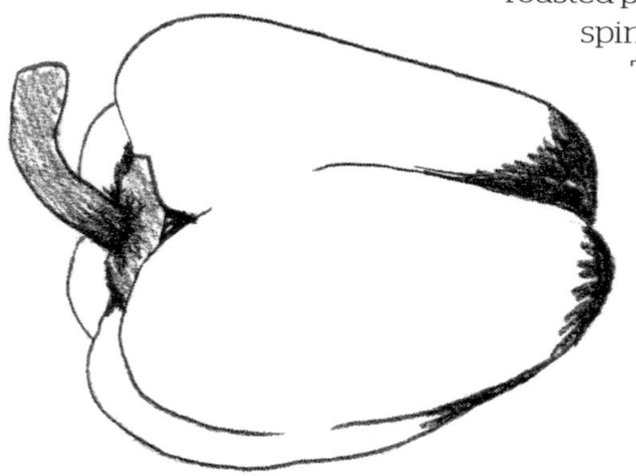

Carrot, Courgette, Orange and Sesame Salad

This salad is really good with fish or as part of a mezze. It is Middle Eastern in influence and flavour: sweet, slightly sour and fragrant. I like this as it is, but you could also put a pinch of powdered cinnamon in the dressing, or add a handful of roughly chopped coriander. Sometimes I throw a handful of sultanas in the dressing and leave them to plump for 30 minutes or so before mixing it all in with the carrots.

Using a sharp knife, cut the peel and white pith away from two of the oranges, then chop the flesh into 1cm cubes. Put the orange cubes in a large serving bowl with the grated carrot and courgette. Lightly toast the sesame seeds in a dry frying pan over a medium heat – this only takes moments and they can burn fast so keep moving them around in the pan – and scatter over the salad.

Finely grate the zest of the lemon into a small bowl, then add the juice of half the lemon and the remaining orange. Whisk together with the orange blossom water, sugar, salt and plenty of freshly ground black pepper. Taste, and add a touch more lemon juice if you think it needs it. Pour the dressing over the salad and toss gently so everything is combined, then cover and leave for a few hours for the flavours to mingle and develop.

Ingredients

3 big juicy oranges
2 large carrots, peeled and grated
1 large courgette, grated
2 heaped tablespoons sesame seeds
1 unwaxed lemon
3 tablespoons orange blossom water
1 – 3 tablespoons caster sugar (depending how sweet you like it)
½ teaspoon of salt
freshly ground black pepper

Curried Chickpea and Coriander Salad

This is a really tasty salad, substantial and healthy. Serve with fresh green leaves and toasted pita bread, or as part of a mezze.

Ingredients

2 teaspoons curry powder
2 tablespoons cumin seeds
1 tablespoon cider vinegar
2 tablespoons lime juice
2 teaspoons maple syrup
1 tablespoon olive oil
1 red onion, finely chopped
1 red pepper, roughly chopped
75g raisins
2 x 400g tins chickpeas, drained and rinsed
handful coriander, roughly chopped
salt and freshly ground black pepper

In a dry, hot frying pan, roast the curry powder and cumin seeds until the seeds are a fraction darker and you start to smell the spices. Put them into a small bowl, and whisk with the cider vinegar, lime juice and maple syrup.

Heat the olive oil in a large frying pan, and fry the onion and pepper lightly until just soft. Add the raisins and chickpeas and cook gently for a further 5 minutes. Take off the heat and add the spiced dressing you made at the start, the chopped coriander and salt and pepper to taste.

Stir well and put into a serving bowl, leaving to cool before serving.

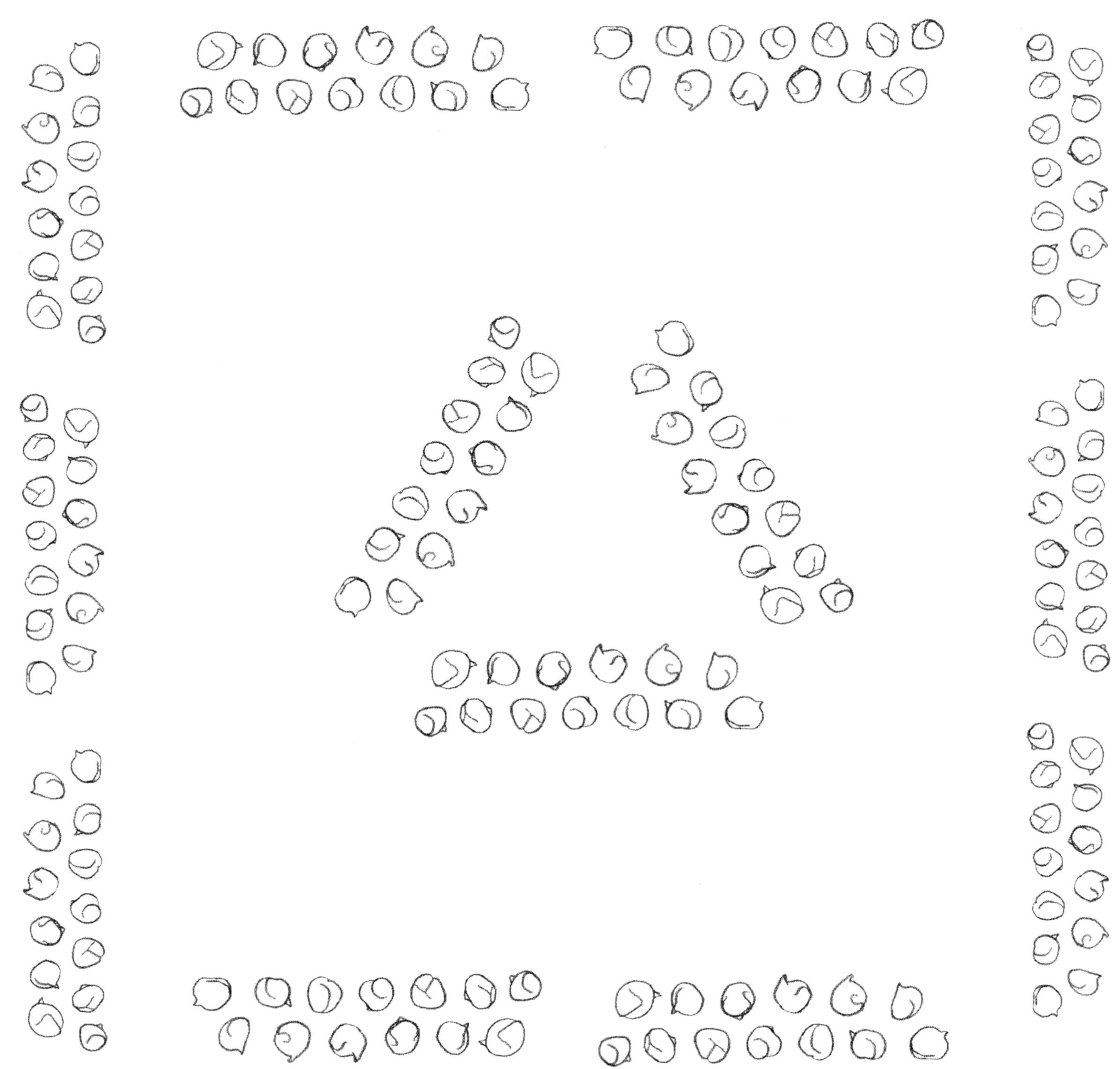

Seasonal Slaw

Home-made coleslaws are a great way to use up left-over vegetables, brilliant for filling wraps for lunch or serving on the side of a summer roast. Here are two of my favourites.

Cabbage, Apple and Honeyed Walnuts

Ingredients

100g walnut halves
1 teaspoon runny honey
250g white or green cabbage, shredded
250g red cabbage, shredded
1 bunch spring onions, finely sliced on the diagonal for more flavour
3 crisp apples, diced or sliced and sprinkled with a little lemon juice
2 tablespoons cider vinegar
2 teaspoons maple syrup
1 teaspoon wholegrain mustard
4 tablespoons olive oil
salt and freshly ground black pepper

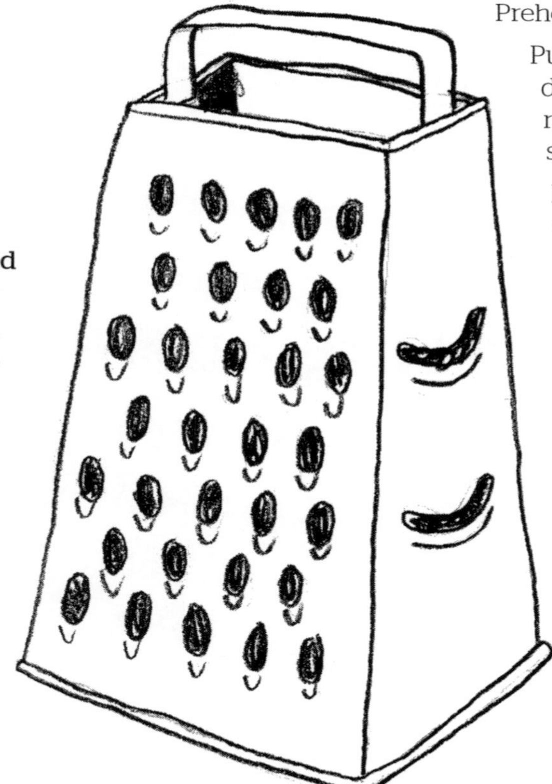

Preheat the oven to 200C.

Put the walnuts on a baking tray and drizzle with honey. Bake for about 7 minutes until they start to brown, then set aside to cool.

In a large serving bowl combine the cabbage, spring onions and apples.

In a small bowl, make the dressing: whisk together the cider vinegar, maple syrup and mustard, then season to taste before whisking in the olive oil.

Stir the dressing into the salad, mix well and add the honeyed walnuts just before serving.

Indian-style Coleslaw

Place the grated carrot, onion, cabbage and sultanas in a large serving bowl. Whisk together the crème fraiche, mayonnaise, lemon juice, white wine vinegar and caster sugar, then add the chilli and ground cumin. Stir into the carrot and cabbage mixture, then scatter with the chopped coriander.

Ingredients

3 large carrots, peeled and finely grated
1 white onion, very finely sliced
500g white cabbage, shredded
150g sultanas (I soak them in hot water for an hour to plump them up)
125ml crème fraiche
125ml good quality mayonnaise
juice of ½ a lemon
1 ½ tablespoons white wine vinegar
1 tablespoon caster sugar
1 chilli, deseeded and finely chopped
1 heaped tablespoon cumin seeds, toasted and ground
handful fresh coriander, finely chopped

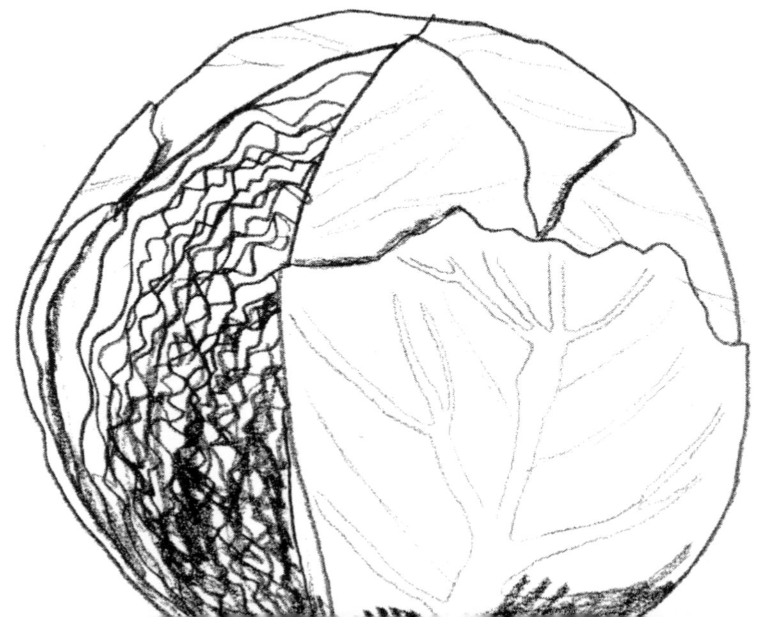

Parlour Panzanella (Bread Salad)

There are loads of recipes out there for this Italian classic, but this is how we like it. It's a brilliant dish for using up old bread and other leftovers – try adding some torn up buffalo mozzarella, or some sliced and cooked spicy Tuscan sausage. We roast our own peppers and use our own tomato sauce, but if you are pushed for time you can use shop bought.

Ingredients

1 ciabatta loaf (approx 270g) or any other rustic style bread
1 small red onion, finely sliced
50ml olive oil
2 tablespoons dried oregano
500g tomatoes, diced
1 bunch spring onions, sliced diagonally
2 tablespoons capers
1 red pepper, roasted, peeled and cut into strips
1 stick celery, chopped
handful pitted olives
handful of basil, roughly chopped
handful of flat leaf parsley, roughly chopped
40ml vinegar (white or red or balsamic or sherry – whatever you fancy or have to hand)
200ml tomato sauce (see page 101)
salt and freshly ground black pepper

Preheat the oven to 190C.

Tear up the loaf into bite-sized pieces and put on a baking tray with the sliced onion. Toss with the olive oil and oregano and bake for 10 minutes.

Meanwhile, put the diced tomatoes, spring onion, capers, pepper, celery, olives, basil and flat leaf parsley in a large serving bowl. Get in there with your hands and mush it all together to get the flavours going and add salt and freshly ground black pepper to taste.

Take the toasted bread out of the oven and immediately sprinkle on the vinegar – you should hear it sizzle. Tip the contents of the baking tray into the tomato sauce, and then mix through all the other ingredients.

This is good served with either some simply dressed rocket alongside or with rocket mixed through it.

Orzo Pasta, Chargrilled Broccoli and Pepper Salad

This is a great salad, hot or cold, really set apart by the chilli, basil and cashew nut pesto dressing. I love orzo – it's a rice shaped pasta available from most ethnic grocers (and increasingly from larger supermarkets too) which is brilliant in salads, and great in soups too as it holds its shape and keeps a good texture. Ideally you need a ridged cast iron grill pan for this, but at a push you could put the broccoli and peppers under a very hot grill.

Cook the orzo in boiling salted water according to the instructions on the packet – it usually takes 12 minutes or so.

Whilst this is cooking you can do the broccoli. It's really important to cook it correctly as the chargrilling won't work otherwise. So, half fill a large saucepan with salted water and bring to the boil. Cut the broccoli into florets (I keep the stalks for soup bases) and drop into the boiling water for 2 minutes. Then drain and plunge the florets into a bowl of ice cold water and leave for 5 minutes. Drain again, and set aside to dry in the colander.

Once the pasta is cooked, drain it, rinse in cold water and set aside until you're ready to assemble the salad. Get the chargrill pan nice and hot, cut the peppers into strips and grill until tender, turning as they start to blacken. Set aside to cool, then dry off the broccoli florets thoroughly and chargrill them in the same way.

In a large serving bowl, gently toss together the orzo, peppers, broccoli, whole cashew nuts and basil. Place all the ingredients for the pesto in a blender and blitz til smooth, then dollop onto the salad, mixing gently, and season to taste.

Ingredients

200g dried orzo pasta
1 large head of broccoli
2 red peppers
50g unsalted cashew nuts, toasted
handful of fresh basil, leaves only
salt and freshly ground black pepper

Pesto
90g parmesan, grated
2 red chillies, deseeded
25g unsalted cashew nuts, toasted
2 large handfuls fresh basil
zest and juice of 1 unwaxed lemon

Chopped Salad with Tahini Dressing

This is another salad full of Middle Eastern flavours. Sumac is a reddish, slightly sour spice made from dried berries: it is used in place of lemon juice all over the Middle East and adds a subtle flavour and colour to salads and meat dishes. It's also great sprinkled over roast chicken once it comes out of the oven.

Ingredients

200g cooked chickpeas, drained and rinsed
40g sultanas
2 pickled gherkins, chopped up small
6 radishes, sliced
2 medium tomatoes, cut into 1cm dice
½ cucumber, cut into 1cm dice
3 spring onions, sliced
2 tablespoons fresh mint leaves, chopped
2 tablespoons tahini
2 tablespoons lemon juice
1 tablespoon olive or groundnut oil
2 tablespoons water
1 teaspoon sumac
salt and freshly ground black pepper

Mix the chickpeas, sultanas, gherkins, radishes, tomatoes, cucumber and spring onion together in a salad bowl and season with salt and a good grind of black pepper. Stir in the mint. To make the dressing, put the tahini in a small bowl. Add the lemon juice and oil, mix well, then slowly add the water stirring all the time until you achieve a consistency like single cream. You may need a little more water – see how it looks.

Toss the salad in the dressing, check for seasoning and then sprinkle with sumac.

Tarts & Pastries

Everybody loves tarts and pastries, don't they? They work really well for us at lunch time: a slice with a couple of salads is about as good a light lunch as a person can have. They look impressive, but they are very simple to do – all you need to master with a tart is the filling and the pastry, and with such great shop-bought pastry around, that just leaves you with the filling to think about. You can use shop-bought pastry for all the recipes in this section and they'll be as delicious – just make sure you get a good brand, preferably one that uses 100% butter. But making your own is a bit like making your own bread – really not that hard – and it's kind of pleasing to know you've made the whole tart, from scratch, in all its crumbly glory.

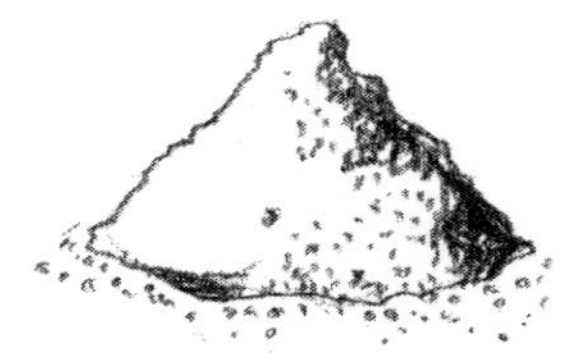

Shortcrust Pastry

This makes 170g, enough for any of the tart recipes in this section. For pain-free pastry making, just remember to keep everything cool, yourself included, and to work it all as lightly as possible. For sweet pastry, add a tablespoon of sugar and leave the salt out.

Ingredients

125g plain flour
55g butter, cubed
1 – 2 tablespoons cold water
salt

Put the flour into a bowl with a pinch of salt, then put in the butter and use your fingertips to lightly rub it into the flour so no big lumps remain. You're aiming for a texture like coarse breadcrumbs – try to work quickly so it doesn't get greasy.

Using a knife, stir in just enough water to bind the pastry together – start with a tablespoon and see how you go. Then wrap the dough in cling-film and leave to rest in the fridge for at least 15 minutes.

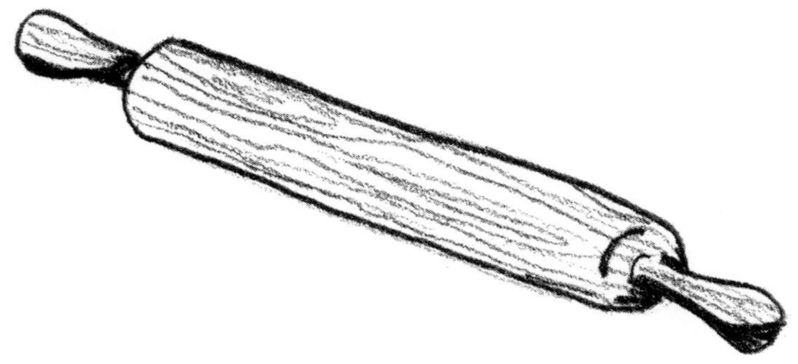

Fig, Gorgonzola and Rocket Tart

Preheat the oven to 190C and put a baking tray in to heat up.

Put a baking sheet in the oven to heat up, then roll out the pastry onto a lightly floured surface and line your tart case. Prick the base all over with a fork, cover with a piece of greaseproof paper and some baking beans (any dried bean will do) and put on the hot baking tray in the oven. Bake for 15 minutes before taking it out to cool (discarding the paper and beans).

Put the onions on another baking tray, drizzle with the olive oil and roast for 20 minutes.

In a mixing bowl, beat the ricotta with the thyme, lemon zest and juice and the egg and yolks. Season well with salt and freshly ground black pepper. Spread the rocket out evenly on the cooled pastry case (it will almost fill it, but that's ok, it cooks right down again) and pour over the ricotta mixture.

Break up the gorgonzola with your fingers and scatter it over, and then arrange the roasted onion and figs artfully or randomly on top, pressing them lightly in. Season lightly and bake for 25 minutes, or until the tart is puffy and golden. Best served warm (not hot) or at room temperature.

Ingredients

1 quantity shortcrust pastry (see page 70) or a 250g packet
2 red onions, divided into eighths
1 tablespoon olive oil
150g ricotta cheese
3 sprigs thyme, leaves only
zest and juice of 1 unwaxed lemon
1 whole egg and 2 yolks, beaten
100g rocket
250g creamy Italian gorgonzola
3 ripe fresh figs, quartered
salt and freshly ground black pepper

also...

10" tart tin, greased

Caramelised Onion and Wholegrain Mustard Tart

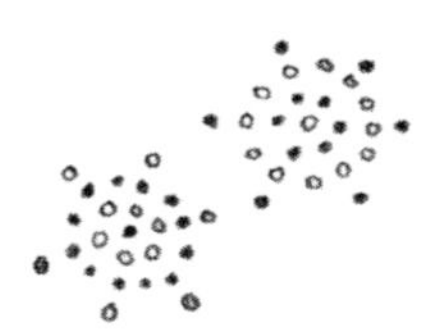

Ingredients

30g butter
2 tablespoons vegetable oil
4 large white Spanish onions, thinly sliced
1 tablespoon good quality wholegrain mustard
2 sprigs thyme, leaves only
4 eggs and 2 egg yolks
200ml double cream
1 quantity shortcrust pastry (see page 70) or a 250g packet
salt and freshly ground black pepper

also...

10" loose bottomed tart tin, greased

Preheat the oven to 220C.

Heat a heavy bottomed pan, large enough to fit all the onions in, and melt the butter and oil together. Then add the onions and cook gently until meltingly soft and sweet. This will take at least 45 minutes: the longer they cook for, the sweeter they get. Take care not to burn them – start on a medium heat and lower it by degrees as they get darker in colour. The finished onions will be dark golden, and soft enough to cut with a spoon. Take the onions off the heat and allow to cool, then add the mustard and the thyme leaves and season well.

Roll the pastry out on a lightly floured surface – you need it large enough to fit into the prepared tart case with an overlap of about 2cm all round. Brush off any excess flour and gently fit the pastry into the tart case, then prick all over the base with a fork. Put a piece of baking paper over the top, weigh down with a handful of baking beans (any dried bean will do) and bake for 10 minutes before removing the beans and the greaseproof paper and returning to the oven for a further 5 minutes. Then reduce the oven temperature to 190C.

In a large bowl beat the eggs, yolks and cream together, then add the onions and combine well. Pour the onion and egg mixture into the cooked tart case, and bake for 20 minutes, or until the top is golden and still slightly wobbly.

Butternut Squash and Feta Empanadillas

These are little crescent-shaped pies from Spain, like miniature Cornish pasties. Great for parties, great for kids, and the pastry is incredibly easy and forgiving so it's a good place to start if the whole notion of pie-making makes you nervous.

Preheat the oven to 220C.

First of all, make the pastry. Sift the flour and salt into a bowl, add the butter and rub in with your fingertips until it starts to look like breadcrumbs. Add half of the beaten egg and stir with a fork to combine, then slowly add the water and keep stirring until the dough comes together in a ball. Go slowly with the water – depending on the size of your egg you may not need it all. Knead lightly, cover and leave to rest in the fridge for at least 15 minutes (you can leave it longer if you need to).

To prepare the filling, put the squash on a roasting tray, toss with 2 tablespoons of the olive oil and roast for 20 minutes or so. Heat the remaining tablespoon of olive oil in a large frying pan and fry the onion and garlic until soft and translucent, then put them into a bowl with the roasted squash and the feta. Give it a good stir to mix, then add the basil and a good grind of black pepper and mix again.

Turn the oven down to 180C. Roll out the pastry nice and thin on a very generously floured work top, then use a glass or a cutter to cut out 12 rounds (more if you can get them) of about 9cm in diameter. Put a heaped tablespoon of the filling on one half of each circle of pastry, then brush the edge with water and fold the pastry over to form a little half moon shaped pasty. Use a fork to crimp and seal the edges. Brush the finished empanadillas with the remaining beaten egg and put in the oven on your oiled baking sheets for 15 to 20 minutes, or until they are golden and delicious looking.

Ingredients

175g plain flour
¼ teaspoon salt
85g butter, cut into 1cm cubes
1 egg, beaten
50ml tepid water
200g butternut squash, peeled and cut into 1cm cubes (about half a squash)
3 tablespoons olive oil
1 red onion, finely chopped
2 large cloves garlic, finely chopped
80g feta, crumbled
8 basil leaves, finely chopped
freshly ground black pepper

also...

2 baking trays, lightly oiled

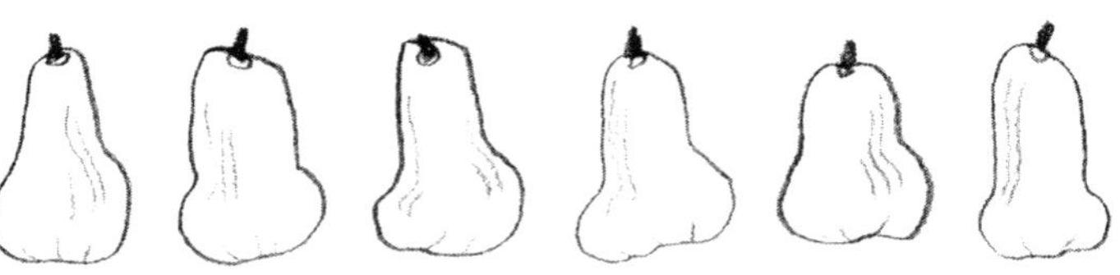

Arbroath Smokie, Leek and Cheddar Tart

You can use a couple of smoked haddock fillets (undyed, not the bright yellow variety) instead of Arbroath Smokies, but it won't be quite as special. So if you can get Smokies you should definitely search them out.

Ingredients

375g all butter puff pastry
1 pair Arbroath Smokies
200ml milk
200ml double cream
2 bay leaves
knob of butter
2 large or 3 medium leeks, chopped
3 eggs and 3 yolks
100g good strong cheddar, finely grated
3 tablespoons freshly chopped chives
salt and freshly ground black pepper

also...

12" flan case, lightly buttered.

Preheat the oven to 220C.

Roll out the puff pastry on a lightly floured surface so it's large enough to fit the flan case with an overlap of about 2cm over the edges. Gently ease the pastry into the flan case, then line with a sheet of greaseproof paper and a handful of baking beans (any dried beans will do). Bake for 10 minutes, then take out the paper and the beans, prick the base all over with a fork and put it back in the oven for 5 minutes to get a bit of colour. Once the pastry case is out, reduce the oven to 190C and put in a baking tray to heat up.

Meanwhile, put the Smokies in a wide pan with the milk, cream and bay leaves. Cover and bring up to a very slow simmer for 15 minutes, then remove the Smokies and bay leaves and allow the liquid to cool. Melt the butter in a small pan and gently fry the leeks until soft and tender.

Flake the flesh of the Smokies, discarding any bones you come across. Measure out 200ml of the fish-infused milk and cream and beat with the eggs and yolks. Season with a pinch of salt (Smokies are quite salty so go easy) and lots of freshly ground black pepper. Now to assemble the tart: first put the cooked leeks in a layer over the pastry base, then flake the Smokies over the top (this gives you a chance to catch any bones you missed first time around). Pour over the egg mixture, then scatter with the cheese and chives.

Put the tart on the hot baking tray in the oven, and bake for 20 to 25 minutes until golden and slightly risen and set in the middle. If the pastry starts to burn, cover with foil for the last 10 minutes of cooking.

Salmon Pithiviers

This looks fantastic as the centrepiece of a buffet, and everyone is always impressed with a big pie. The crème fraiche and ricotta keep the salmon juicy; the tarragon and mushrooms give a wonderful flavour – all in all, it's a perfect party dish.

Preheat the oven to 220C.

In a large saucepan, melt half the butter and gently fry the onion and garlic until soft and translucent. Add the mushrooms and fry until everything is tender and any liquid has evaporated, then stir in the crème fraiche and the tarragon. Remove from the heat and place in a bowl to cool. When cool, stir in the ricotta and the parmesan and season with salt and plenty of black pepper. In the same pan you cooked the onions in, melt the remaining butter and sauté the spinach until it has wilted. Squeeze and drain off any excess liquid and season with salt, pepper and nutmeg.

Cut the pastry in two, one piece slightly bigger than the other, and roll the smaller piece into a rectangle (just big enough to fit the fillet of salmon on top). Put it on a lightly greased baking sheet, prick all over with a fork and bake for 10 minutes.

Place the salmon on the cooked pastry (trim the edges of the pastry to fit, leaving a border of 1cm), then sprinkle over the lemon juice and season lightly. Top with a layer of spinach and then a layer of the mushroom mixture. Roll out the remaining pastry large enough to fit right over the salmon, and then dampen the edges of the cooked pastry. Drape the uncooked pastry over the salmon and seal by pressing down around the edges with a fork. Trim any excess to make a nice neat parcel. Brush the whole thing with beaten egg, make a couple of slashes on the top to let steam escape, and bake in the middle of the oven for 25 minutes. If the pastry browns too much, cover with foil for the last few minutes of cooking. Spectacular.

Ingredients

65g butter
1 large onion, finely chopped
1 clove garlic, finely chopped
125g chestnut mushrooms, roughly chopped
75ml crème fraiche
2 tablespoons tarragon, chopped
125g ricotta
2 tablespoons parmesan, grated
450g baby spinach
pinch of nutmeg
450g all butter puff pastry
700g middle salmon fillet, skin removed
juice of ½ a lemon
1 egg, beaten
salt and freshly ground black pepper

σπανακόπιτα

Spanakopita Filo Pie

I sometimes add a handful of sultanas and some toasted pine nuts to the filling, but it's pretty good as it is. You could also use olive oil instead of melted butter to brush between the leaves of filo if you like it a little lighter. Great served with a simple tomato salad and some tzatziki.

Ingredients

4 tablespoons olive oil
1 medium onion, finely chopped
2 garlic cloves
500g baby spinach
3 eggs, beaten
100ml double cream
125g ricotta cheese
125g feta, crumbled
2 sprigs thyme, leaves only
juice of ½ a lemon
270g filo pastry
50g melted butter for brushing the pastry
salt and freshly ground black pepper

also...
8" cake or deep tart tin

Preheat the oven to 190C.

You need to make the filling first and only open the pastry when you are ready to put the pie together and cook it. So, firstly, heat up the olive oil in a large frying pan. When it's hot, gently cook the onion and garlic until they are soft and translucent – about 5 minutes. Add the spinach and cook with a lid on over a medium heat until it has wilted, then transfer to a colander to drain off any excess liquid. In a large bowl, beat the eggs with the double cream, ricotta and crumbled feta, then stir in the spinach and onion mixture, thyme leaves and lemon juice and combine well. Add a pinch of salt and a good grind of pepper.

Now brush your tin with melted butter – a springform one is the easiest to use. Open the filo pastry and take out half, wrapping the rest up in cling-film for now. Start to layer up the filo sheets to make the base of the pie. Use 8 sheets, brushing a little butter in between each, and you should end up with a lot of pastry overlapping the edges of tin – you need to work quite quickly so the pastry doesn't dry up. Pour the spinach cheese filling into the pastry case, then fold over the excess pastry to make a lid to the pie (it doesn't matter if it doesn't completely cover it). Get the remaining sheets of pastry out of the packet and, working with a sheet at a time, brush it with butter, scrunch it up in your hand and place it on top of the pie. It should look like filo flowers (sort of!). Now brush the whole thing lightly with butter and place in the oven for about 25 minutes, by which time the pastry will be crisp and golden. Unclip the cake tin and transfer the pie (still on the base, for ease) onto a large plate to serve. It will look beautiful!

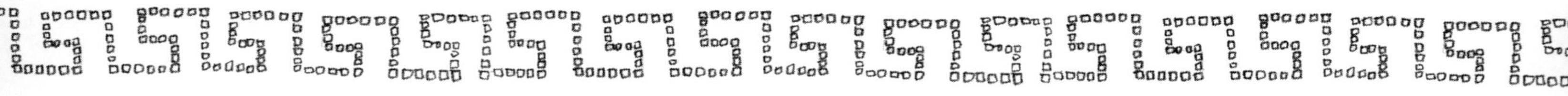

Sweet Potato, Chorizo and Goats Cheese Tart Tatin

Though these are really easy to make, there's something incredibly impressive about individual tarts. This is a great dinner party starter, and it makes a lovely lunch with some salad.

Preheat the oven to 200C, and put in a baking tray large enough to hold all the tart tins to heat up.

Bring a large pan of water to the boil, then put in the sweet potato and cook until just tender (10 minutes or so should do it). Take the cubes out of the water using a slotted spoon and leave them to cool in a colander, then put the shallots into the same water to boil for another 10 minutes. Drain and leave to cool.

In a small pan heat the sugar and butter on a medium high heat, stirring constantly, until the sugar melts to a dark caramel. Take off the heat and pour the caramel evenly on the bottom of each of the four tins. Now arrange the sweet potato, shallot and chorizo on the caramel, scatter with thyme leaves and lay a slice of goats cheese on the top. Roll out the pastry quite thin – about 5mm – and cut into 4 circles a couple of centimetres wider than the diameter of the tart tins. Place one over each tin, tucking the excess under the sweet potato/shallot layer.

Put the tarts in the oven on the hot baking tray and bake for 15 minutes, then turn down the heat to 180C and bake for another 5 to 10 minutes. The tarts are ready when the pastry is risen and golden brown. As soon as they're out of the oven, turn them out onto a plate to serve.

Ingredients

1 medium sweet potato, cut into 1.5cm cubes
200g shallots, peeled and halved lengthways
80g caster sugar
20g butter
4 small cooking chorizos, cut into 1cm slices
4 sprigs thyme
4 slices chevre goats cheese
250g puff pastry
salt and freshly ground black pepper

also...

4 individual 10cm tart tins, lightly oiled

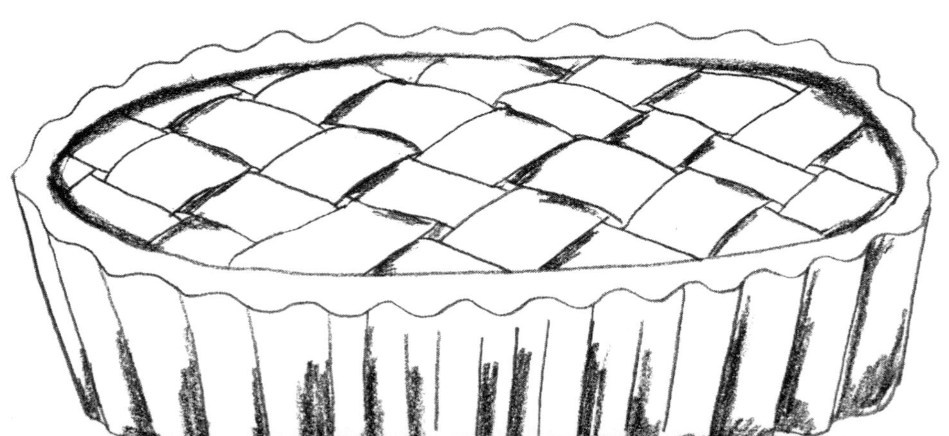

Mains

These are all big-in-flavour, big-in-size, stand-alone dishes that are great for dinners and parties. We always have a couple on in the café for customers who really want to get stuck in, and they fly out of the kitchen. At home I pull them out when I've got friends coming round and will usually bang them on the table with a well-dressed green salad and a couple of bottles of wine. What else do you need?

Aubergine Parmigiana

This is a great dish for a dinner party and, in the unlikely event you have any left over, tastes totally fantastic the next day. I like to serve it on its own with garlic bread, but it is also a good accompaniment to meat or fish.

Ingredients

4 large aubergines
100ml olive oil
20 vine tomatoes
2 teaspoons icing sugar
375g mozzarella balls
30g basil leaves, stalks removed
70g parmesan
1 batch tomato sauce (see page 101)
salt and freshly ground black pepper

Preheat the oven to 220C.

Heat a couple of large baking trays in the oven. Cut the aubergines into 2cm slices widthways. Toss the slices in 5 tablespoons of the olive oil until they are all glistening. Season with salt and freshly ground black pepper, and space them out on the hot oven trays, making sure they have enough room. Put them in the oven and bake until browned (20 minutes should do it).

Cut the tomatoes in half and scoop out the seeds with a teaspoon. Toss them in the remaining olive oil, season and put onto hot oven trays as for the aubergines. Douse in sieved icing sugar for that sweet sensation and bake for 20 minutes.

Reduce the oven to 180C.

Cut the mozzarella balls into thinnish slices. Spread some of the tomato sauce over the base of a large, deep, oven-proof dish (at home I use an oval one about 30 x 20cm and 6cm deep).

Once the aubergines and tomatoes are out of the oven and have cooled, start building your parmigiana. Start with a layer of aubergine, then tomato, then mozzarella and basil and repeat, finishing with a layer of mozzarella.

Now place some more dollops of tomato sauce loosely over the top and sprinkle generously with shavings of parmesan.

Bake for 30 to 40 minutes until golden and bubbling.

(depending how big you like them)

Parlour Bean Burger

We've been making these burgers as long we've been open, and they're as popular now as they ever were. Don't expect dry breadcrumby patties – these are loose and juicy and soft, more like veggie sloppy joes. Try them between two flat-breads with roasted garlic and caper mayonnaise and a spoonful of red onion marmalade (see page 105).

Firstly, in a hot pan add a tablespoon of olive oil, then fry the mushrooms and garlic over a high heat. Keep a close eye on the pan, and lower the heat as they start to brown – you want to caramelise the mushrooms to intensify the flavour, but not burn them. Once done, set aside to cool.

Into a large bowl, put all the drained and rinsed beans, soy sauce, coriander and parsley. Use a hand blender to mash everything together but don't completely turn it to mush as you want a bit of texture. Now add the mushrooms and combine, adding salt and pepper as needed. Divide the mixture into 4, and form each quarter into a flat round patty about 1cm thick. (You could do all this in advance, and then leave the burgers covered on a plate in the fridge until you're ready to eat.) Heat a little oil – just a tablespoon will be enough – in a non-stick frying pan over a medium heat, and then fry the burgers until they're browning on the outside and hot all the way the way through (3 minutes each side should do it). Be gentle as you turn them over.

You can keep these warm in the oven or reheat if not using straight away.

Ingredients

2 tablespoons olive oil
250g closed cup or chestnut mushrooms, finely chopped
1 large clove garlic, finely chopped
300g cooked black eyed beans (tinned are fine)
300g cooked pinto beans (tinned are fine)
2 tablespoons dark soy sauce
1 tablespoon flat leaf parsley, finely chopped
1 tablespoon fresh coriander, finely chopped
salt and freshly ground black pepper

Roasted Sweet Potato, Mushroom and Pepper Stack with Goats Cheese and Tarragon Sauce

Ingredients

- 2 large red peppers
- 2 sweet potatoes, peeled and sliced into 1cm thick discs
- 4 large Portobello mushrooms
- 200ml tarragon sauce (see page 104)
- 4 slices chevre goats cheese
- olive oil for frying and roasting

Preheat the oven to 180C.

First roast the peppers – either put them in the oven until the skin is charred all over (about 45 minutes), or place under a hot grill and keep turning as the uppermost sides blacken. Either way, once done, put the peppers in a bowl and cover with cling-film. When cool you should find the skin peels off easily, then remove the stalk and the seeds and cut each pepper into halves.

Heat a large frying pan with a tablespoon of olive oil and fry the sweet potato slices on both sides until they are a little crispy and golden in colour. Transfer to a baking tray, season with salt and pepper and roast in the oven until tender throughout (20 to 25 minutes should do it).

The Portobello mushrooms can go in the oven at the same time – just place them on a baking tray drizzled with a little olive oil, salt and pepper.

While that's all roasting, you can get on with the sauce. Once the vegetables are cooked, take them out of the oven and turn it up 190C. Lightly oil a baking tray and then build your 4 stacks on it. Start with a base of sweet potato (depending on the size of the potato, I'd normally use about 3 slices to form a wide base). Then put on a Portobello mushroom (stalk side down), top with a roasted pepper half and, finally, lay a slice of goats cheese on the top. Bake for 10 to 12 minutes until the goats cheese is soft and starting to bubble, and serve immediately with the warm tarragon sauce spooned over.

This doesn't need much more than a nice, crisp green salad.

Chorizo and Chickpea Stew

You need the uncured, raw or cooking chorizo for this (which is stocked in most supermarkets).

Ingredients

3 small cooking chorizos (about 150g)
250g small waxy potatoes, halved
2 tablespoons olive oil
1 large onion, chopped
1 carrot, chopped
handful of fresh thyme
2 bay leaves
5 garlic cloves, finely chopped
1 teaspoon turmeric
1 tablespoon smoked paprika
2 x 400g tins of tomatoes
3 tablespoons white wine
1 – 2 tablespoons sugar
400g tin chickpeas
1 – 2 tablespoons sherry vinegar
salt and freshly ground black pepper

Preheat the oven to 240C.

Put the chorizos on a baking tray and roast in the hot oven. Drizzle the potatoes with a tablespoon of the olive oil on another tray, and put them in to roast also. Be careful to turn the chorizo every few minutes and remove when it's a nice brown colour – it burns very easily. Once cooled, cut into chunky slices. Take the potatoes out when they're tender and crisp – about 30 minutes.

Meanwhile, heat the remaining tablespoon of oil over a medium heat in a large saucepan and, when it's hot, put in the onion, carrot, thyme, bay leaves and garlic. Fry until everything is soft and golden. Sprinkle over the turmeric and paprika and cook for a minute, stirring, then add the tomatoes, the white wine and a tablespoon of the sugar and bring to the boil. Reduce the heat and leave to simmer gently. Once the liquid is reduced by about a third (about 20 minutes), stir in the drained chickpeas and simmer, covered, for another 15 minutes.

By now the stew will have thickened to a lovely juicy, jammy consistency. Add the roasted chorizo and potatoes and simmer again on a low heat for 10 to 20 minutes to allow the flavours to merge. If it starts to look a bit dry, add a splash of boiling water.

Pick out the thyme stalks and bay leaves and add a tablespoon of vinegar. Taste and add a touch more vinegar or sugar as you think it needs it – you're looking for the perfect balance of sweet and sour.
Season with salt and a good grind of black pepper.

Vegetable and Apricot Tagine

This is an easy one pot dish, so make sure you have a heavy bottomed pan that is large enough for all the ingredients. To toast the cumin, dry fry the seeds in a small frying pan until they turn a shade darker, then grind in either a mortar and pestle or a coffee grinder.

Ingredients

1 large onion, finely chopped
2 tablespoons olive oil
1 small aubergine, cut into 1 cm cubes
2 tablespoons tomato purée
1 teaspoon ground cinnamon
1 teaspoon cumin seeds, toasted and ground
400g tin tomatoes
350ml vegetable stock
1 large sweet potato, cut into 1cm cubes
200g swede, cut into 1cm cubes
125g semi-dried apricots
1 fresh red chilli, finely chopped
3 tablespoons ground almonds
1 teaspoon runny honey (optional)
handful of flat leaf parsley, chopped

Firstly, start to cook the onion in the oil until soft and translucent, then add the aubergine and fry until it has softened. Add the tomato purée, cinnamon and toasted and ground cumin and carry on frying until everything begins to brown and you can smell the spices.

Stir in the tin of tomatoes and the vegetable stock, then add the sweet potato, swede, apricots and chilli. Add a little water until everything is just covered. Bring to the boil and simmer gently, with a lid on, for about 45 minutes or until the vegetables are almost tender, then stir in the ground almonds and cook for another 5 minutes. Finish off with the teaspoon of honey if you're using it, and scatter with the flat leaf parsley.

All you need with this is some couscous or fresh, crusty bread.

Spicy Ratatouille

This is a really handy and flexible dish to have in your repertoire – excellent on its own with some good bread and cheese, great to fill our brunch crêpes (see page 20) or to serve with some boiled rice if you want something more substantial. You can chuck in some chickpeas or cannellini beans to up the protein, or crack a few eggs on top and simmer, covered, for another 10 minutes to cook the eggs.

Ingredients

2 sweet red peppers
3 tablespoons olive oil
1 large aubergine, cut into 2cm cubes
1 large onion, halved and sliced
3 large cloves of garlic, sliced
1 small red chilli, finely chopped
1 courgette, sliced
3 sprigs of thyme
4 plum tomatoes, peeled and chopped (tinned are fine)
1 teaspoon smoked paprika
handful of basil leaves
salt and freshly ground black pepper

Preheat the oven to 180C.

Roast the peppers on a baking tray in the oven for about 20 minutes (you only want to soften them). Meanwhile heat 2 tablespoons of oil in a large saucepan, add the aubergine and cook, stirring from time to time, on a medium heat until the aubergine softens and starts to brown.

While that's cooking, warm a tablespoon of the oil in a frying pan and sweat the onion until it is soft and transparent. Turn the heat to low, add the sliced garlic and the chilli and leave to fry gently for another 10 minutes. Add the courgette and the thyme to the pan of softened aubergine and cook for a further 15 minutes, before stirring in the chopped tomatoes, smoked paprika and the cooked onions. Remove the stems and seeds from the roasted peppers, cut them into 1cm slices and add into the pan.

Simmer gently for 20 minutes or so – once it has come together as a pulpy stew, season with salt and pepper and add the freshly torn basil leaves.

Gorgonzola, Red Onion Marmalade, Spinach and Pine Nut Roulade

This is a rich dish, which is great for special occasions. I've provided some lighter suggestions for lunches and (as it travels well) picnics.

Preheat the oven to 200C.

First line a 9 x 13" baking tray with greaseproof paper. Leave a rim of paper around the edges – about 3 to 4 centimetres all around.

In a large bowl beat the egg yolks, parmesan, 100g of the cream cheese, the leaves from 2 of the thyme sprigs and half of the flat leaf parsley. Season with salt and black pepper. In another bowl whisk the egg whites into stiff peaks, and then gently fold them into the egg and cheese mixture, keeping it all as light as possible (using a metal spoon helps). Gently pour the mixture onto the lined baking tray, spreading it into an even layer with the back of a spoon, then bake for 12 minutes or until puffy and golden.

Whilst the roulade is cooking, start on the filling. With a fork, mix the remaining 200g of cream cheese, the gorgonzola, the cooked and shredded spinach, the remaining thyme and flat leaf parsley and season to taste with salt and pepper. If the mixture is looking very thick, you may want to loosen it with a little hot water to make it spread more easily.

Once the roulade is ready, take it out of the oven and allow to cool. Cover it with a sheet of greaseproof paper, and then put another baking sheet on top so you can flip the roulade over. Peel off what is now the top sheet of greaseproof paper.

Gently spread the Gorgonzola filling all over the roulade, cover with red onion marmalade and then sprinkle on the pine nuts. Then taking one end of the greaseproof paper, roll the roulade like a big Swiss roll, easing away the paper at the same time.

Because this is quite rich, I think it goes well with a simple salad or some tenderstem broccoli lightly dressed with lemon juice and good olive oil.

Ingredients

5 eggs, separated
50g parmesan, finely grated
300g cream cheese
4 sprigs of thyme, leaves only
large handful of flat leaf parsley, finely chopped
200g creamy Italian gorgonzola
200g baby spinach, cooked, squeezed dry and chopped
250ml red onion marmalade (see page 105)
handful of pine nuts, lightly toasted
salt and freshly ground black pepper

Here are some other fillings that work really well:

- *crispy smoked bacon, caramelised leeks and cheddar*
- *goats cheese, roasted pepper and wilted spinach*
- *stilton, black pudding and apple*
- *roast squash, feta and roast tomatoes*

Twice Baked Cheddar and Red Onion Potatoes

This dish can be as decadent or as light as you wish, and here's the decadent version. To make it lighter, use low-fat crème fraiche instead of cream and low-fat butter and cheese and then just eat less of it... Half a potato makes a good side dish; a whole one with salad makes a great lunch.

Ingredients

4 medium to large baking potatoes, pricked all over
2 tablespoons maple syrup
1 red onion, finely sliced
200g very strong cheddar, grated
40g salted butter, diced
100ml double cream
4 eggs, beaten
salt and freshly ground black pepper

Preheat the oven to 190C.

Put the potatoes on a baking tray and bake for about 1¼ hours, then brush them all over with the maple syrup and return to the oven for another 15 minutes.

Once the potatoes are out of the oven, cut completely in half and scoop out the insides into a mixing bowl. Mash them up with a fork, add all the other ingredients and give it a really thorough mix. Lay the empty potato shells on the baking tray and fill them up with the mashed potato mixture, then put them back in the oven for around 15 to 20 minutes until nicely browned.

Other things you can fill them with:

- ***goats cheese instead of cheddar, with a dollop of our red onion marmalade (see page 105)***
- ***add some smoked bacon, fried or grilled until crispy***
- ***add some leeks that have been softened in butter, then loosened with a bit of double cream or crème fraiche***
- ***mix the potato with wilted spinach and crumbled stilton.***

Aubergine Stuffed with Spinach, Feta, Harissa and Mint

Cut the stalks off the aubergines, then slice lengthways into 5mm slices. In a small pan, gently heat the oil and garlic until bubbles appear, then turn off the heat and leave to infuse for a minute or so. Put a griddle pan on a high heat and, while it's getting hot, brush the slices of aubergine on both sides with garlic oil. Then griddle the aubergine slices for a few minutes on each side and lay out on a large baking tray or flat dish.

Crumble the feta into a bowl with the harissa, parsley, mint, pine nuts and spinach and mix well. Spoon a little of this filling onto each slice of aubergine and roll up, securing with a skewer if need be, and arrange on a serving plate as the centrepiece of a mezze.

Ingredients

2 medium aubergines
125ml olive oil
2 garlic cloves, grated to a pulp
200g feta cheese
2 tablespoons harissa (see page 98)
40g flat leaf parsley, finely chopped
10g fresh mint, finely chopped
60g pine nuts, lightly toasted
200g spinach, wilted
and squeezed dry
freshly ground black pepper

Dressings, Sauces & Flavourings

This is where you go the extra mile: put a bit of time and a lot of love into your sauces and dressings and it will transform what you do in the kitchen. I'm really big on salad dressings – you can't beat a green salad with a good dressing on it – and, as usual, once you've got the technique worked out, you can use them to play around with flavours. Always use the best olive oil you can get, use fresh herbs, buy some decent vinegar and experiment with different kinds. The sauces in this section are all very versatile and can lift a simple dinner into something much more stellar – home-made hollandaise, for example, is a doddle, and it tastes really special on eggs or with the first of the season's asparagus dipped into it.

Basic Salad Dressing

Ingredients

1 tablespoon white wine vinegar
1 tablespoon lemon juice
1 large clove garlic, peeled and crushed
1 teaspoon Dijon mustard
1 teaspoon runny honey
6 tablespoons olive oil
salt and freshly ground black pepper

Put the vinegar, lemon juice, garlic, mustard and honey into a screw top jar and shake well to combine. Taste and add salt and pepper as you think it needs it, then pour in the olive oil and shake again until the dressing emulsifies. This keeps in the fridge for a good few days, but let it come up to room temperature and shake well before serving.

Pomegranate and Basil Dressing

A great punchy salad dressing, also terrific on grilled lamb. You can buy pomegranate juice in most supermarkets and delis.

There are two ways of making this.

You can either put the lemon juice, mustard, garlic, pomegranate juice and basil in a screw top jar and give it a good shake. Season to taste and add the olive oil, then shake again until the dressing emulsifies.

Or, even easier, you can just stick everything in a small jug and blitz with a hand blender until smooth, adding a pinch of salt and a good grind of freshly ground black pepper at the end.

Ingredients

1 tablespoon lemon juice
½ teaspoon Dijon mustard
2 small garlic cloves, crushed
4 tablespoons pomegranate juice
8 leaves fresh basil, finely chopped
125ml olive oil
salt and freshly ground black pepper

Honey, Orange and Sesame Dressing

Ingredients

juice of 1 orange
1 teaspoon finely grated orange zest
2 tablespoons balsamic vinegar
1 teaspoon runny honey
1 teaspoon sesame seeds, lightly toasted
5 tablespoons olive oil
salt and freshly ground black pepper

Whisk up the orange juice, zest, balsamic vinegar, honey and sesame seeds with a pinch of salt and some black pepper. Taste and adjust the seasoning if you need to, then slowly whisk in the olive oil.

Balsamic, Honey and Mustard Dressing

Ingredients

4 tablespoons balsamic vinegar
1 heaped tablespoon runny honey
1 teaspoon wholegrain mustard
1 sprig of thyme, leaves only
1 small garlic clove, finely grated
4 tablespoons olive oil
salt and freshly ground black pepper

In a small bowl, whisk together all the ingredients apart from the olive oil, and season. Once you're happy with the balance of flavours, slowly whisk in the oil until the dressing is emulsified.

Hollandaise Sauce

We use this on our poached egg muffins at the weekends, either with some salmon, a thick slice of roast gammon or over wilted spinach and mushrooms. Delicious.

Ingredients

8 peppercorns
1 bay leaf
3 tablespoons white wine vinegar
2 egg yolks
125g butter
½ teaspoon lemon juice
salt and freshly ground black pepper

Put the peppercorns, bay leaf and vinegar into a small pan and boil hard to reduce by two thirds. Strain into a bowl – you should have only a tablespoon left.

Place the egg yolks in a blender with the vinegar reduction.

Melt the butter very gently over a low heat and you will see all the milk solids gather at the bottom of the pan. Take the butter off the heat and cool for about 40 seconds, then start to blend the eggs and vinegar whilst pouring in the butter in a very slow but steady stream (take care to leave the milk solids in the pan). You may not need all of it: keep a close eye as the sauce starts to thicken – you don't want it as thick as a shop-bought mayo, just thick enough to coat the food you're going to pour it on, so stop pouring when it looks like the right consistency.

Once the hollandaise is thick enough, season with lemon juice, a pinch of salt and a good grind of black pepper.

Roasted Garlic and Lemon Aioli

This stuff's amazing – delicious with chorizo or any other spicy sausage, or with pan-fried mushrooms. It's also great on our bean burger, with a few finely chopped capers stirred in.

Ingredients

1 garlic bulb
100ml vegetable oil
90ml olive oil
1 egg yolk
½ tablespoon Dijon mustard
juice of 1 lemon
salt and freshly ground black pepper

Preheat the oven to 200C.

Start with your roasted garlic – you might as well do a whole bulb as it's so good, even just spread on toast. Slice the very top off a bulb of garlic so you can see in all the cloves, then wrap it loosely in tin foil and roast for 30 minutes until it's soft and golden.

Stir the two oils together in a measuring jug. Then squeeze 2 big cloves of the roasted garlic out of their skins and into the bowl of your food processor, along with the egg yolk and mustard, and process until smooth. With the motor still running, add the oil very slowly, drop by drop. Once the aioli starts to emulsify, you can accelerate to a slow steady stream until all the oil is used up. Slowly add the lemon juice (take it easy – you may not need it all and you don't want the aioli to be too thin) and add a touch of salt and freshly ground black pepper to taste.

Salsa Verde

This is great as a dressing for salads or potatoes and excellent with fish. This recipe makes enough to use in our Pan Bagnat (see page 34), but it will keep for about 5 days in the fridge so you may want to double it up.

Simply pulse everything in a food processor until you achieve the consistency you like.

I like to make sure all the herbs are completely chopped but there is still an interesting texture to the sauce.

Check for seasoning and add more oil if it needs loosening a little.

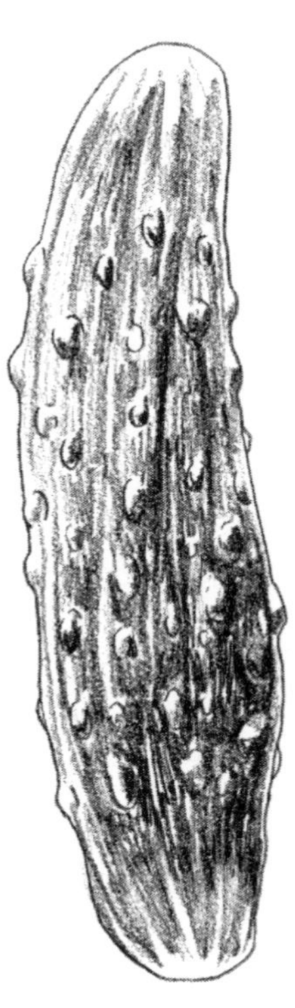

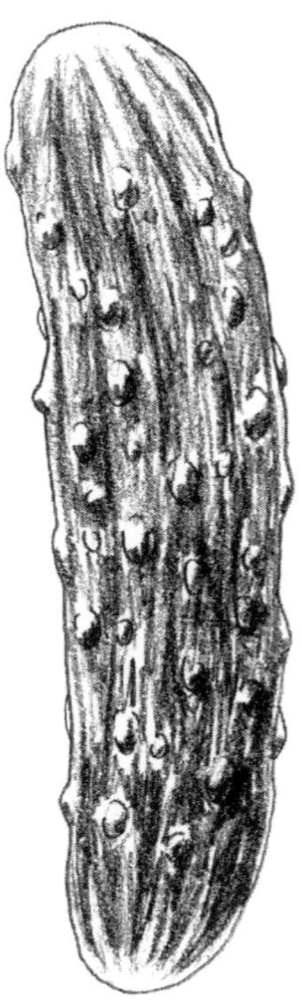

Ingredients

4 shallots, roughly chopped
2 garlic cloves, roughly chopped
20g basil
40g Italian flat leaf parsley
juice and zest of 1 unwaxed lemon
2 tablespoons capers
3 medium pickled gherkins
30g breadcrumbs
125ml olive oil
freshly ground black pepper

Harissa

This Moroccan paste is great to mix with couscous or stir into soups and stews, and it is fantastic rubbed into potatoes before roasting. You can adjust the heat depending what kind of chillies you use.

Ingredients

1 teaspoon caraway seeds
1 teaspoon coriander seeds
½ teaspoon cumin seeds
12 dried chillies
1 roasted red pepper, peeled and stalk and seeds discarded
4 cloves garlic
½ teaspoon salt
4 teaspoons olive oil

Toast the caraway, coriander and cumin seeds in a dry, hot frying pan for a few minutes, and then grind roughly with a mortar and pestle. Put into the blender with all the remaining ingredients and blitz to a thick smooth paste. Store in an airtight jar in the fridge.

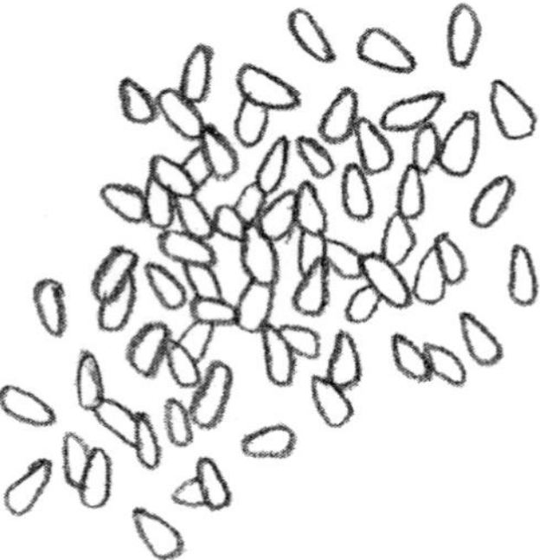

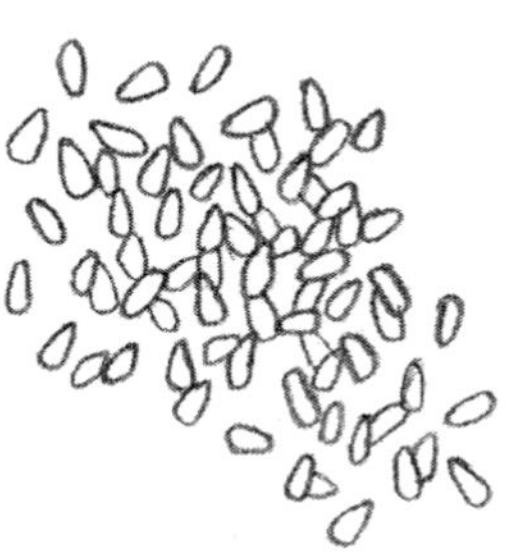

Rocket and Walnut Pesto

This recipe is adapted from Scot Herbs' samphire pesto recipe but substitutes rocket (which is more readily available) for the samphire. It's delicious stirred into pasta, in sandwiches, or as a pizza or coca bread topping.

Set the oven to 180C, and put in the walnuts on a baking tray while it is heating up. They should be toasted in 5 or so minutes.

Put the toasted walnuts, rocket, garlic, oil and lemon zest in a blender and blitz to a rough paste for about 20 seconds. Just before serving, beat in the parmesan and add salt and freshly ground black pepper to taste.

If you're not using it immediately, freeze it without the cheese, or put it in the fridge with a layer of olive oil on top to prevent the pesto browning. To serve, bring it up to room temperature and beat in the cheese just before you want to eat.

Ingredients

60g walnuts
100g rocket, rinsed and dried
3 garlic cloves, roughly chopped
125ml best quality extra virgin olive oil
zest of ½ an unwaxed lemon
30g parmesan or pecorino cheese, coarsely grated
salt and freshly ground black pepper

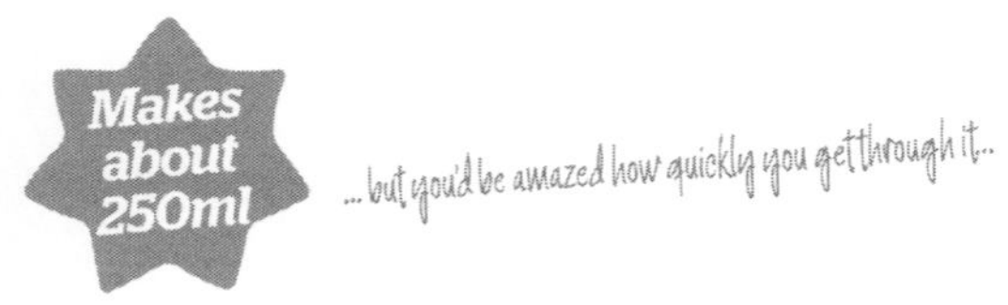

Garlic Butter, Parlour Café Style

A crucial ingredient in our griddled bread recipes, this also makes amazing garlic bread, is great on sweetcorn and perks up any potato or spinach dish. And try putting a bit of the butter, cold from the fridge, on a just-grilled steak.

Ingredients

230g softened butter
1 heaped tablespoon minced garlic
1 tablespoon vegetable oil
1 teaspoon dried oregano
1 teaspoon freshly ground black pepper
1 egg yolk
¼ teaspoon unwaxed lemon zest, very finely grated
a pinch of salt

Put all the ingredients into a blender and blitz to form a smooth butter. Store in an airtight container in the fridge.

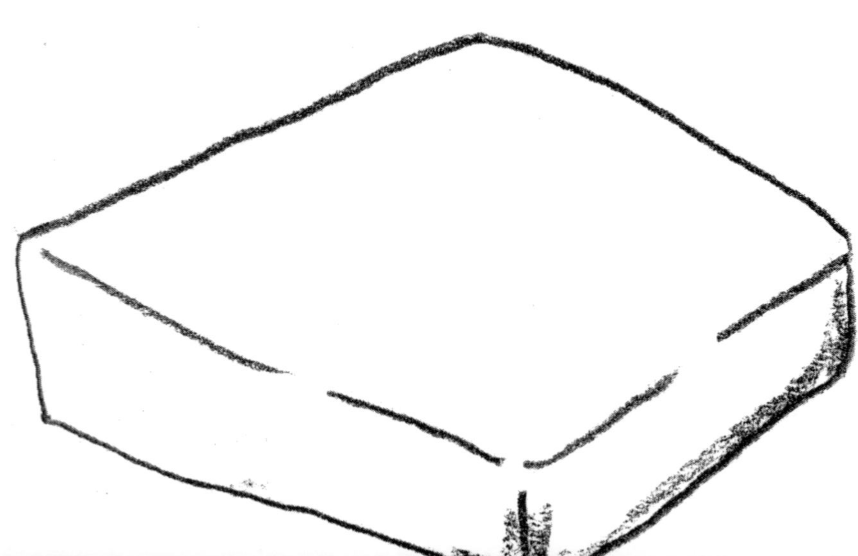

Tomato Sauce

This is very useful: you can use it as a simple sauce for pasta, in a vegetarian lasagne, to stuff vegetables, to add to soup or as a pizza sauce. I like to dip good bread in it.

It keeps so well in the fridge (about a week) or the freezer (indefinitely) that you may as well make a big batch – it doubles or even triples up really easily. This amount makes about twice what you need for our Aubergine Parmigiana, so you could have that one night and keep the rest for an easy pasta dinner for 2 some other time.

If you have some string, tie the thyme and bay leaves neatly together before putting into the pan, and it will be easier to remove them at the end. And if you like your tomato sauces really garlicky, separate and peel all the garlic cloves before adding them and blend along with everything else at the end.

Ingredients

2 tablespoons olive oil
2 small onions, finely chopped
1 large carrot, diced
handful of fresh thyme
a few bay leaves
1 whole head of garlic
800g chopped tomatoes (2 x 400g tins)
1 tablespoon Worcester sauce
1 tablespoon sugar
1½ – 2 tablespoons red wine vinegar
salt

Heat the olive oil in a large saucepan over a medium heat. Once it's hot, put in the onions, carrot, thyme, bay leaves and the whole head of garlic and give a good stir, then fry until everything starts to take on a nice golden brown hue. Add the tomatoes, Worcester sauce and half of the sugar and bring to the boil, stirring regularly. Turn down the heat to low, half cover and simmer for 1 to 2 hours – the longer the better. Stir every so often to ensure the sauce does not catch and burn.

Once most of the liquid has evaporated, the vegetables are absolutely soft and the sauce has deepened in colour and amalgamated nicely, stir in 1½ tablespoons of the red wine vinegar and season with salt. Simmer for a few more minutes and taste, adjusting with more vinegar, sugar or salt if necessary. Leave to cool, then pick out the whole garlic head, thyme and bay leaves before blending the sauce in a food processor or with a hand blender.

Easy Cherry Tomato Compote

This makes a delicious side dish for brunch or lunch, and is also good to dip bread into or on top of a bruschetta.

Ingredients

50g butter
50g sugar
300g cherry tomatoes
2 sprigs basil
½ red onion, finely chopped

Put everything in a pan and cook over a medium heat for 15 minutes. Like it says, easy. Serve hot or at room temperature.

Béchamel Sauce

Or white sauce – one of the most useful sauces you can make.

Ingredients

1 small onion, ends cut off and peeled
4 cloves
300ml milk
1 bay leaf
5 peppercorns
15g butter
15g plain flour
a pinch of nutmeg
salt and freshly ground black pepper

Stud the onion with the cloves and put into a small saucepan with the milk, bay leaves and peppercorns. Bring to a simmer, remove from the heat and allow to infuse for 15 minutes or so before straining into a jug.

In another saucepan, gently melt the butter (be careful not to burn it) and stir in the flour thoroughly. Cook for a couple of minutes, then gradually pour in the milk, stirring continuously over a low heat. Season with a pinch of salt, freshly ground black pepper and nutmeg. Up the heat to medium and keep stirring until the sauce is thick and smooth. If there are any lumps, don't panic, just give it a whisk and they should disappear.

To make a cheese sauce, add a teaspoon of mustard powder with the flour and, once the sauce is finished, take it off the heat and stir in around 50g of strong cheddar.

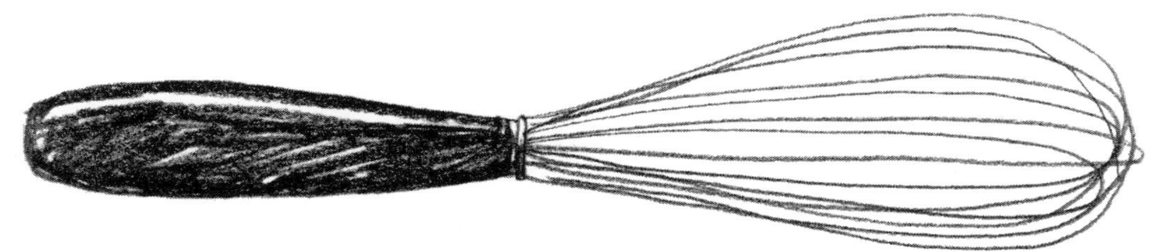

Tarragon Sauce

In the café we serve this with the Roasted Sweet Potato, Mushroom and Red Pepper Stack, but it is also brilliant with poached salmon or a baked chicken breast.

Ingredients

10g butter
olive oil
1 small onion, finely chopped
100ml white wine
juice of ½ a lemon
200ml double cream
20g fresh tarragon, finely chopped

In a small saucepan, melt the butter with a drop of olive oil over a lowish heat, then gently fry the onion until it's soft and translucent but not coloured.

Add the wine and the lemon juice, raise the heat and boil until reduced down to a couple of tablespoons of liquid. Add the cream and the tarragon and boil again to reduce by a third.

You can leave it as it is, slightly textured, or use a hand blender to blend until it's smooth.

Red Onion Marmalade

I don't see the point in making a little of this as it keeps for weeks in a sealed container in a fridge and has a multitude of uses. In the café we serve it with our bean burger and on pastrami sandwiches, but it's also fantastic with cheese and a good topping for Coca Bread. And it makes a great present.

Ingredients

6 tablespoons olive oil
1kg red onions, sliced
40g caster sugar
40g dark soft brown sugar
1 teaspoon fresh thyme
zest and juice of 1 orange
140ml leftover red wine
175ml sherry vinegar

In a heavy bottomed pan heat the oil over a medium heat and then add the sliced onions. Give them a good stir, coating them in the hot oil, and soften for around 10 minutes. Add both lots of sugar, thyme and orange zest, and keep stirring until all the sugar has melted and the onions are starting to caramelise.

Turn the heat down and cook for a further 40 minutes, keeping an eye that it doesn't start to burn. The onions should be very soft and break up easily when you press them with a spoon. Now add the orange juice, red wine and vinegar and simmer very gently until most of the liquid has evaporated and you are left with the onions in a dark sticky sauce.

Take the marmalade off the heat and set aside to cool, then decant into boiled jam or kilner jars.

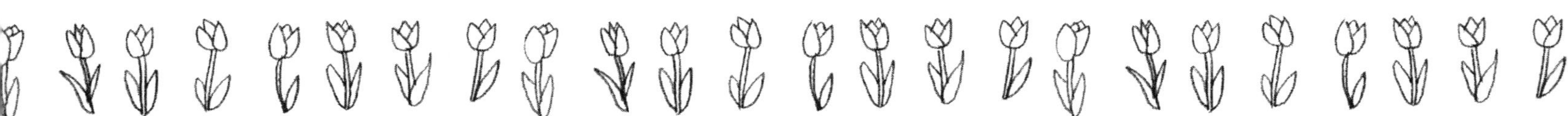

Sweet Pepper and Chilli Jam

This is a good recipe for playing about with – you could use different spices or throw in some tomato, or vary the heat by using more or less chilli.

Ingredients

2 sweet red peppers, deseeded and cut into ½cm strips
1 red chilli, finely chopped and half the seeds discarded
80g caster sugar
250ml water
110ml white wine (or sherry) vinegar
½ teaspoon mustard seeds
½ teaspoon coriander seeds
2 cardamom pods, lightly crushed with the back of a knife

Put all the ingredients into a heavy bottomed saucepan and bring to the boil, then turn down to a simmer and cook for 20 minutes or so.

Take off the heat and use a hand blender to blitz roughly (keep a bit of texture). The jam will thicken as it cools.

Decant into boiled jam or kilner jars.

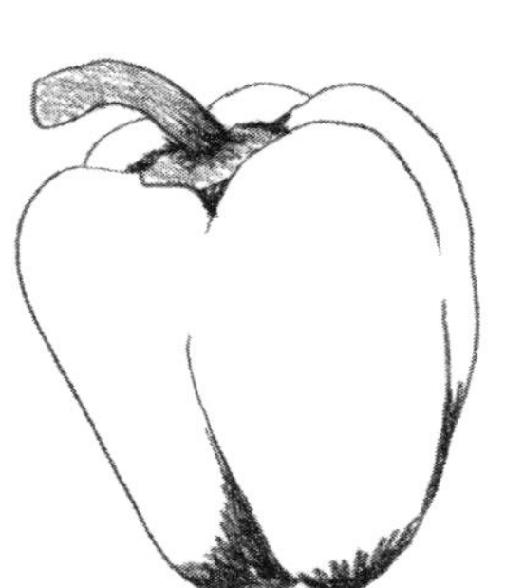

Sweet Things

What a lot of people really love about a café is an excuse to go and have a piece of cake. It's hard to resist a counter full of sweet stuff, and we don't hold back on our cakes, muffins and biscuits – they look beautiful, taste even better and will always be big, and moist, and crumbly. But there's nothing better than having something home-made, and all this stuff is as fun to make as it is to eat.

I'm not the best pastry chef in the world, so a lot of the recipes that I make are very forgiving – everything here is pretty much foolproof. As ever, the quality of the ingredients counts: use large, free-range eggs (at least, if not organic), and the best butter and darkest chocolate you can get hold of.

Alison at the Yellow Door Bakery also makes a lot of stuff for us and, as a highly trained pastry chef, she takes the whole thing to another level. Her cakes are the stuff of legend, and she's kindly passed on a few of her most popular recipes here.

Parlour Baked Cheesecake

This is a classic baked cheesecake, made a bit fresher with the addition of some sharp yoghurt and a touch of lemon juice. It serves 6 – 8, but it's very easy to double up and make for a big party. Just use a slightly bigger tin (10" is about right), use the same quantities for the base ingredients (biscuits, tablespoon of sugar and butter) and then double up on everything else. Totally delicious on its own, but it would also be great served with a handful of soft fruit.

Ingredients

150g digestive biscuits
150g + 1 tablespoon caster sugar
100g butter, melted
575g cream cheese at room temperature
1 teaspoon lemon juice
1 teaspoon vanilla essence
40g natural yoghurt
pinch of salt
3 eggs and 1 yolk

also...
8" springform cake tin

Preheat the oven to 160C.

Get the base started first: crush the biscuits (either with the end of a rolling pin in a sturdy bowl, or in a food processor) and add the tablespoon of sugar and half of the melted butter. Brush the base of your cake tin with some of the remaining butter, then cut and fit a disk of greaseproof paper to line it. Brush more butter on the paper. Press the biscuit mix in an even layer in the tin and bake for 10 to 15 minutes, then cool on a wire rack. Once cool, brush the sides of the tin with the last of the butter.

Turn the oven up to its highest setting. For the filling, beat the cream cheese together with the remaining 150g of sugar, lemon juice, vanilla, yoghurt and a pinch of salt in a large mixing bowl. In a separate bowl, roughly whisk the whole eggs and extra yolk and then gradually incorporate them into the cheese mix, beating as you go. Pour into the prepared tin and put into the oven on a baking sheet.

Bake for 10 to 15 minutes and, once the edges have started to turn golden brown, turn the oven down to 105C and bake for a further 45 minutes to 1 hour. The cheesecake is ready when it is firm to touch but still wobbles lightly upon shaking.

Take out of the oven and cool on a wire rack before unclipping the tin and putting the cheesecake on a pretty plate to serve.

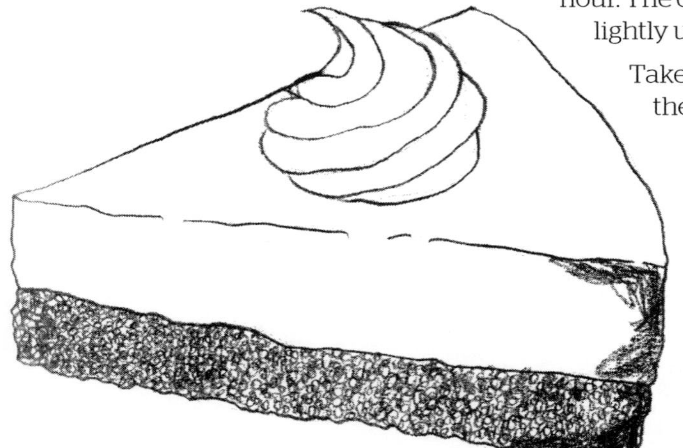

Parlour Chocolate Cake

Clearly, one look at the ingredients will tell you that this isn't an everyday chocolate cake. But it is an amazing one, and well worth making when you want to pull out all the stops for a special occasion. It flies out of the café whenever we make it.

It may look complicated, but it's actually pretty easy to make – just take your time and make sure you use your biggest mixing bowls. This makes two cakes, which you can either ice separately or sandwich together. You can easily halve the recipe and just make one, but the cakes freeze beautifully, so if you don't want the full sandwich cake you could ice one and put the other in the freezer, ready to pull out when the occasion presents itself.

Preheat the oven to 160C.

Start with the cakes. Break up the chocolate, put it with the butter in a heatproof bowl over a bain-marie and leave to melt, stirring along the way. Once it has all melted, take the bowl off the heat and allow to cool a little.

Get out two large mixing bowls (the biggest you've got) and separate the eggs, putting the yolks in one bowl and the whites in the other. Begin whisking the egg whites with an electric mixer. Once they have increased two to three times in size, gradually add in 300g of the sugar, continuing to whisk for up to 10 minutes until you have glossy white peaks. Whisk the remaining sugar with the yolks until pale and foamy. Add the melted chocolate to the yolk/sugar mix, fold in gently with a metal spoon, and then fold in the flour. Stir a spoonful of the whites into the chocolate mixture to loosen it, then pour in the rest of them and fold together using a smooth cutting action, rotating the bowl as you combine. Do not rush this – make sure that the chocolate from the base of the bowl is combined and any lumps of white are fully incorporated. Pour the batter into the two tins – they will seem very full but don't worry, the cakes puff right up while baking but then sink a lot as they cool. Bake for 30 to 40 minutes, or until a skewer inserted into the centre of the cake comes out with only a few damp crumbs clinging to it. Leave the cakes in their tins on a wire rack, only turning them out when fully cool.

For the icing, break the chocolate into pieces and melt with the butter over a bain-marie. Warm the cream in a small pan and add to the melted chocolate, then add the syrup and stir gently until silky smooth. Leave to cool until the icing is thick enough to coat the back of a spoon. Use this to ice the middle, top and sides of the cakes, levelling and coating the sides with a palette knife.

Ingredients

Cake

500g dark chocolate, min. 60-70% cocoa solids
500g salted butter, sliced
12 eggs, separated
400g caster sugar
100g plain flour

Icing

400g dark chocolate, min. 60-70% cocoa solids
250g unsalted butter, sliced
100ml double cream
2 teaspoons golden syrup

also...

2 x 10" springform tins, brushed with melted butter, lined, and brushed with butter again

Carrot Cake with Citrus Cream Cheese Icing

One of Yellow Door Bakery's classic cakes: this is a lovely, light cake made with sunflower oil (instead of butter) and whisked egg whites. You can also use the same quantity of grated raw beetroot for a change. Once iced, you need to store the cake/ buns in a tin in the fridge, but it will keep for up to 5 days.

Ingredients

Cake

500g caster sugar
360ml sunflower oil
4 very large eggs
1 teaspoon vanilla essence
2 tablespoons water
330g self raising flour
1 tablespoon mixed spice
¼ teaspoon bicarbonate of soda
¼ teaspoon baking powder
200g carrot, grated
40g unsweetened desiccated coconut
150g chopped nuts (use any you like or have in the cupboard)
50g raisins (optional)

Icing

250g unsalted butter, softened (take it out of the fridge 1 – 2 hours beforehand or stick it into the microwave for 30 seconds or so)
375g icing sugar
zest of 2 oranges
zest of 1 unwaxed lemon
250g cream cheese

also...

2 x 9" cake tins, lined and greased

Preheat the oven to 165C.

In a large bowl (or a food mixer fitted with a paddle attachment) beat together the sugar, oil, 2 of the eggs and the 2 remaining egg yolks. Save the whites for later in the recipe. Add the vanilla and the water and whisk until the mixture is pale and smooth – about 5 minutes with a hand whisk, 2 minutes with an electric one or food mixer. In another bowl, sift together the flour, mixed spice, bicarbonate of soda and baking powder and fold it lightly into the egg mixture. Then fold in the carrot, coconut, nuts and raisins (if you're using them). Take the 2 egg whites you saved from earlier and whisk them until they're bulky and floppy but not stiff, then fold them into the batter. Spoon into the cake tins and bake for 45 to 50 minutes until golden and risen (poke a toothpick into the middle and when they're done the toothpick should come out clean). Cool the cakes in their tins on a wire rack.

For the icing, beat the butter in a large bowl, then add the icing sugar by degrees, beating after each addition. When the butter cream is pale, fluffy and smooth, beat in the orange and lemon zests. Soften the cream cheese with a spoon (go easy, you don't want it too soft, just loose enough to stir), then add the butter cream bit by bit until it's all combined. Sandwich the cakes together with a good thick layer of the icing, and spread some more on the top.

You can make buns with this too – just line 12 muffin tins, spoon in the mixture and bake for 25 to 30 minutes.

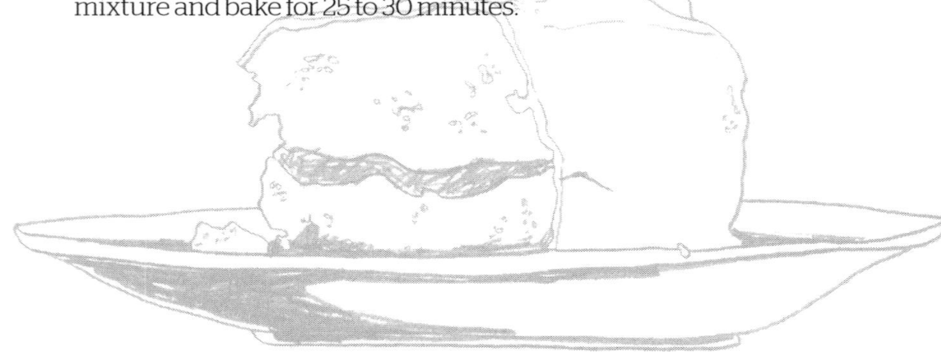

Satsuma Cake

Preheat the oven to 190C.

Place the satsumas or clementines, skin and all, in a large pan of water and bring slowly to the boil. Simmer for 2 hours, covered, turning occasionally so the fruit cooks evenly. Drain and cool. Cut the fruit in half, remove all the pips and purée with a blender.

Whisk the eggs in a bowl and add in the sugar, mixing well until light and foamy, then stir in the puréed fruit. Mix the baking powder with the ground almonds and sieve onto the egg mix. Give it a good stir to combine, then pour the batter into the prepared tin and bake for around an hour. The cake is done when it is golden and springy to touch, and the edges are pulling away from the tin.

Sprinkle with a little caster sugar and leave to cool for 10 minutes before gently removing from the tin, carefully releasing the sides with a knife if need be. Leave to cool fully on a wire tray before serving.

Ingredients

375g satsumas or clementines
6 eggs
225g caster sugar
1 heaped teaspoon baking powder
250g ground almonds

also...
8" springform cake, tin brushed with melted butter and lined with greaseproof paper

Serves 8

Banana Bread with Coconut and Toasted Nuts

This started life as The Magnolia Bakery banana bread recipe, but Alison the cake lady has given it a few twists and made it her own. It stores brilliantly – if you're not eating it that day, take out of the tin and peel off any greaseproof paper, then wrap in clean paper and cling-film It'll keep in a cake tin for 5 to 7 days or can be frozen.

Ingredients

80g chopped nuts (any kind you like)
6 tablespoons corn oil (vegetable will do fine)
170g caster sugar
2 medium eggs
6 tablespoons double cream
1½ teaspoons vanilla essence
2 large bananas
1 tablespoon lemon juice
215g plain flour
1½ teaspoons bicarbonate of soda
¾ teaspoon salt
¾ teaspoon cinnamon
40g desiccated coconut

also...
1lb loaf tin, lightly oiled or lined with greaseproof paper

Preheat the oven to 165C.

Spread the nuts on a baking tray and bake in the heating-up oven until lightly toasted. In a large bowl whisk together the oil, sugar, eggs, cream and vanilla essence. In another bowl, mash the bananas with a potato masher or fork and add the lemon juice. Sieve the flour, bicarbonate of soda, salt and cinnamon into the oil and sugar mix and stir until just absorbed. Then add the mashed bananas, toasted nuts and coconut and mix in thoroughly.

Pour the batter into the prepared tin (don't worry if it looks a bit empty – the cake will rise to half its size again) and bake for 45 to 60 minutes. After 45 minutes, check for doneness by inserting a wooden toothpick or skewer into the centre of the cake – if it's done, it should come out clean: if not, give it another 5 minutes and check again. Don't be tempted to check before the 45 minutes are up or you run the risk of sinking all your hard work. Leave to cool in the tin on a wire rack before unmoulding.

To make banana muffins, line 12 muffin tins with paper cases and spoon in the mixture. Cook for 25 minutes or until a skewer comes out clean.

Hummingbird Cake

This is another classic American cake, based on the recipe in Nancie McDermott's Southern Cakes and then given the Yellow Door Bakery treatment. The icing is optional – you can just as well use fresh cream or serve it on its own and it will still be as delicious.

Preheat the oven to 165C.

In a large bowl, beat together the oil, vanilla essence, eggs and sugar until well blended. Sieve the flour, bicarbonate of soda, cinnamon and salt and fold into the egg mixture until just combined. Then take another bowl and roughly mash the bananas in it before stirring in the crushed pineapple, its juice and the chopped nuts. Stir the fruit into the cake batter, pour into your prepared tins, and then bake for 50 minutes. When a toothpick comes out clean and the cakes are fragrant and golden, cool in their tins on a wire rack.

At this point you could wrap them in cling-film to freeze or keep in the fridge for up to 5 days, but otherwise, get on with the icing. Put the soft butter in a bowl or a food mixer and start to beat in the icing sugar until it is pale and fluffy. Stir in the vanilla essence. Soften the cream cheese with a spoon, then gently stir it into the butter cream before folding in the pecans or walnuts.

Use half the icing to sandwich the cakes together, and the other half to cover the top. Demolish.

Ingredients

Cake

280ml corn oil
1½ teaspoons vanilla essence
3 eggs
425g caster sugar
450g plain flour
1 teaspoon bicarbonate of soda
1 teaspoon cinnamon
1 teaspoon salt
5 medium bananas
227g tin crushed pineapple (in juice, not syrup)
100g chopped nuts (really, whatever you fancy)

Icing

225g salted butter, softened
350g icing sugar
2 teaspoons vanilla essence
250g cream cheese
75g pecans or walnuts, roughly chopped

also...

2 x 9" springform cake tins, brushed with oil and lined with greaseproof paper

Rhubarb Crumble Muffins

Ingredients

For the crumble topping
60g plain flour
40g ground almonds
40g light soft brown sugar
40g butter, diced

For the muffin batter
350g plain flour
2 teaspoons baking powder
2 teaspoons bicarbonate of soda
1 tablespoon cinnamon
salt
2 large eggs
250g light soft brown sugar
2 tablespoons sunflower or corn oil
1 tablespoon vanilla extract
200ml buttermilk (or 100ml natural yoghurt mixed with 100ml milk)
200g rhubarb, chopped into 5mm chunks

also...
12 muffin tin and paper cases

Preheat the oven to 190C.

First make your crumble topping. Add all the dry topping ingredients into a bowl and then rub in the butter using your fingertips until it resembles coarse breadcrumbs. Set aside.

Now for the muffin batter: sift the flour, baking powder, bicarbonate of soda, cinnamon and a couple of pinches of salt into a large bowl. In another bowl, thoroughly mix the eggs, sugar, oil, vanilla extract and buttermilk (or yoghurt/milk mixture). Once mixed, add the rhubarb. Then add the wet mix to the dry mix and combine. It is important not to over work the batter. Try to combine it in under ten full stirs: it doesn't matter if there are lumps and small pockets of flour, the muffins will be better and lighter for it (that goes for almost all muffin mixes).

Line your muffin tins with paper cases and fill with the batter right to the top, then sprinkle on a layer of crumble topping, pressing it down gently so it doesn't bounce off as the muffins rise. Bake for 20 to 25 minutes or until a skewer poked into the middle comes out clean, and leave to cool on a wire rack.

They're delicious hot or cold, but in the café we like to serve them warm, with crème fraiche on the side.

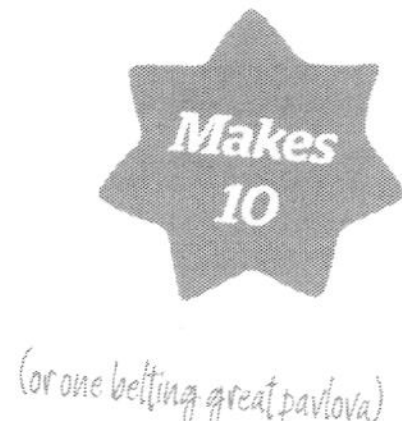

(or one belting great pavlova)

Big Beautiful Meringues

These are truly beautiful, and they're delicious with fresh fruit and cream, or with our lemon curd, or made into a pavlova. If it looks like an odd list of ingredients, don't panic – you basically need to weigh your egg whites and then use double the weight of caster sugar. A couple of tips: really, you need an electric mixer for making meringues – a hand whisk will never get the same results, no matter how long you're at it. And make sure your bowl is scrupulously clean or your egg whites will never ever whisk up – it is harder to get plastic mixing bowls really clean which is why I've recommended you use pyrex here.

Ingredients

5 egg whites
up to 500g caster sugar

Preheat the oven to 100C and line two baking trays with greaseproof paper. Weigh your egg whites and put them in a pyrex bowl. Then weigh out twice the amount of caster sugar, and add it to the egg whites. Set the bowl over a saucepan with about an inch of simmering water in it and stir continuously over a low heat until all the sugar has dissolved. When the sugar has totally melted and the mixture is warm, pour into the bowl of your food mixer (if you're using a hand held electric whisk, just take the bowl off the heat and start whisking in that) and whisk until the mixture is cool to the touch and forms thick, standing white peaks. It'll take about 10 minutes.

Dollop large spoonfuls artfully on the baking parchment and bake for 30 minutes, then leave in the turned-off oven overnight to cool completely. If they still feel a little soft in the morning, you can give them another 15 minutes at 100C.

In the final 10 seconds of whisking, you could add any of the following:

- ***my favourite – a pinch of ground pink peppercorns and a handful of crushed pistachios***
- ***a tablespoon of the best quality cocoa powder***
- ***freeze dried raspberries, crushed to a dust***
- ***roughly chopped almonds.***

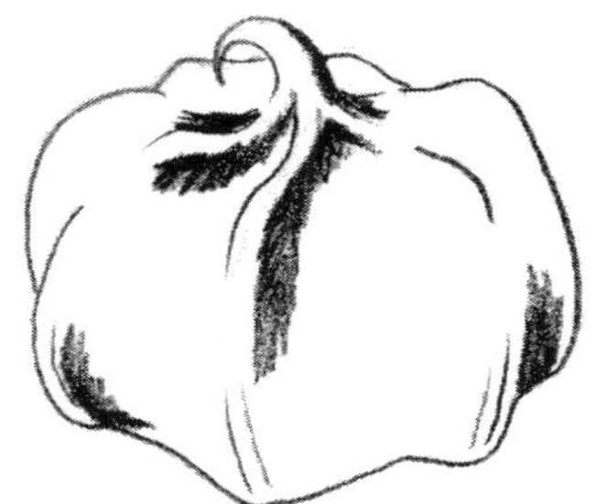

Lemon Curd

Amazing with our meringues, also good added to granola and yoghurt, spread on a warm scone or simply eaten on its own with a spoon...

Ingredients

4 egg yolks
150g caster sugar
60g unsalted butter, cut into 1cm cubes
100ml lemon juice
2 teaspoons lemon zest (use unwaxed lemons)

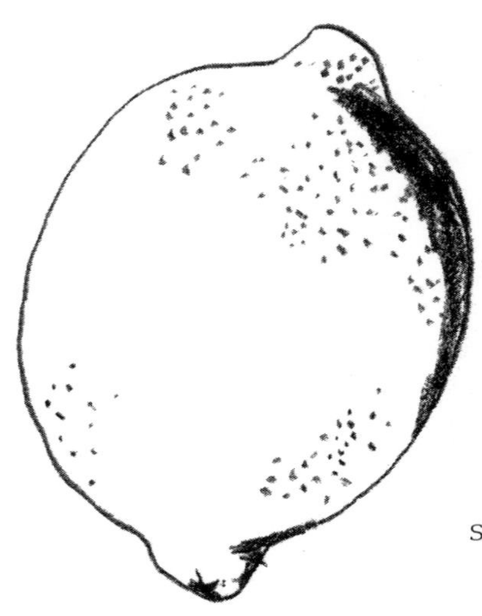

Whisk the egg yolks and sugar together in a bowl until completely combined and foamy, then add the butter, lemon juice and zest.

Set the bowl over a pan with about an inch of simmering water in it, and stir continuously until the mixture thickens. This takes a bit of time (up to 15 minutes), but don't try to rush it and turn the temperature up too high or your curd will end up scrambling – not a good look.

Once it's good and thick, pour the curd into a sterilised jar and keep in the fridge.

Scones

Preheat the oven to 220C.

With your fingertips, rub the flour with the butter until it looks like coarse breadcrumbs. Stir in the sultanas and sugar. In a jug, mix the yoghurt and milk with a fork. Make a well in the centre of the dry ingredients and pour in the yoghurt and milk mixture; give a it good stir until the dough starts to come together. Turn out onto a floured surface.

Knead the dough as lightly as possible until it is soft and not sticky, then flour the top and roll out to about 3cm thick (any thinner and your scones can end up tough). Cut out the scones with a 7.5cm cutter or a wine glass, and when you can't cut out any more, gather up the remaining dough and roll out again. Stagger them on floured baking trays and bake for 15 to 20 minutes.

Put on a wire rack to cool, and eat while still a little bit warm.

Ingredients

450g self raising flour
80g salted butter, cubed
110g sultanas
50g caster sugar
250g yoghurt
60ml milk

Pear, Cinnamon and Almond Cake

Ingredients

150g butter
125g golden caster sugar
1 large egg
150g ground almonds
½ teaspoon almond extract
½ teaspoon cinnamon
175g plain flour
1 teaspoon baking powder
6 tinned pear halves, roughly chopped
60g flaked almonds
honey to drizzle
(or icing sugar for dusting)

also...
8" cake tin, greased and lined

Preheat the oven to 180.

Cream the butter and sugar together until light and fluffy, then break in the egg and beat well to combine. Stir in the ground almonds, almond extract and cinnamon, and then swiftly fold in the sifted flour and baking powder, stirring just until the batter is smooth.

Spread the mixture evenly over the base of the cake tin, then scatter over the roughly chopped pears and the almonds and bake for 35 minutes.

Take the cake out of the oven, and either drizzle with honey while it's still hot or wait until it's cool and sprinkle with icing sugar. It's delicious either way.

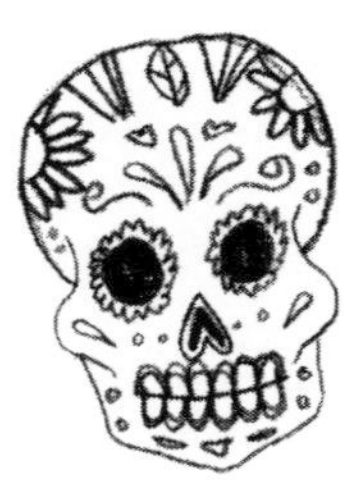

Index

123

D

E

F

G

H

L

M

O

P

Q

R

S

T

V

W